Religious education of the deaf

Modern approaches to the diagnosis and instruction of multi-handicapped children

11

Religious education of the deaf

Proceedings

*of the International Catholic
Conference on Religious Education
of the Deaf, Dublin, July 1971*

Edited by
J. van Eijndhoven

Foreword by
Rev. Br. D. E. Drohan

1973

Rotterdam University Press

The manuscripts were revised by miss Mary J. O'Mahony,
(Conference Administration and Organisation).

ISBN 90 237 4111 0

Printed in the Netherlands

Foreword

International Conferences are very common now-a-days, but this was one with a difference. At International Conferences on the Education of the Deaf over the last decade the question of Religion and the deaf child had been discussed, but never to the complete satisfaction of teachers. The Catholic Teachers felt that there were many problems unsolved which they wished to discuss. One of the suggestions made to help in this respect was to have an International Conference devoted specifically to the question of Religion. The reason for the Catholics choosing to go it alone was, that we need to have our own house in order before we become ecumenical.

A small group of Irish and Dutch teachers got together and planned the Conference. Ireland was chosen as the venue because of fifteen hundred years of unbroken tradition in the Catholic Faith and because Ireland supplies missionaries to many countries throughout the world.

We chose a broad variety of topics for discussion at the Conference which would enable delegates to discuss subjects in the light of their own experience in different cultures. This proved very satisfactory as delegates became aware of the problems facing teachers of the deaf in many countries far different to their own. We all had the basic problem of communicating the Good News to the deaf, as most aids on the market are prepared for use with the hearing person. Usually the language was too difficult and the concepts too abstract.

The papers read at the Conference proved to be very well chosen as they dealt with the problems which cause worry even in the hearing world. The deaf need to be enlightened. The authors of the Papers helped very much to clear our minds and make us aware of what part of the message of Christ we need to get across to the deaf. All our speakers were experts in their own particular field as you will see from reading this book.

We decided to have a Conference on the Religious Education of the deaf, but we wish to make it understood that Religious Education cannot be treated in isolation where the education of a deaf person is concerned. Religion is a way of living, so the subject must be integrated into the whole programme of the education of deaf people.

Our conference was a great success. Credit for this must go to all the willing and helpful teachers of the deaf, not only from the host country, but many others also who helped to make the conference a reality.

The Conference received extensive coverage in the Irish National Press. For this we are very grateful.

The First International Catholic Conference on the Religious education of the Deaf will be remembered for its frankness, cordiality and wonderful spirit.

Br. Dermot E. Drohan

Contents

Contributors

Rev. Fr. P. Bergmann, Principal of the school for the Deaf, Tabora, Tanzania.

Most Rev. Dr. Peter Birch, Bishop of Ossory, Kilkenny, Ireland.

Rev. Fr. Dr. John Cahill, O.P., Professor of Theology at St. Mary's, Tallaght, Co. Dublin, Ireland.

Rev. Fr. John Cleary, C.M., Chaplin to the deaf, St. Peter's, Phibsboro Dublin, Ireland.

Rev. Br. Dermot E. Drohan, Teacher of the deaf. Head of Partial Hearing Department, St. Joseph's school for deaf boys, Cabra, Dublin, Ireland.

Rev. Fr. J. J. M. van Eijndhoven, General Director, Instituut voor Doven, Sint Michielsgestel, The Netherlands.

Rev. Fr. Dermot O'Farrell, C.M., Chaplin to the deaf, 13, Lansdown Crescent, Glasgow, N.W., Scotland.

Right Rev. Mgr. Paul H. Furfey, Professor em. of Sociology at the Catholic University of America, Washington, D.C., USA.

Rev. Sister Nicholas Griffey, O.P., Director, Diploma Course for Teachers of the Deaf, University College, Dublin, Ireland.

Right Rev. Mgr. John P. Hourihan, Archdiocesan Director Apostolate for the Deaf, Mount Carmel Guild, 17, Mulberry St., Newark, New Jersey, 07102, USA.

Professor Armin Lowe, Professor, Institut für Hör-, Sprach- und Sehgeschädigtenpädagogik, Heidelberg, Germany.

Rev. Br. Gerald McGrath, C.F.C., Principal of St. Gabriel's School for the Deaf, Castle Hill, N.S.W. 2154, Australia.

Rev. Fr. Antoine van Uden, Head of Department for research and psychology, Instituut voor Doven, Sint Michielsgestel, The Netherlands.

Statement and resolutions

The handicap of deafness as distinct from all other forms of physical and mental handicap, requires, because of the severe associated communication problem, special consideration and help in close interaction with schools and institutes for the deaf.

Language development and catechetical instruction go hand in hand. Deprivation of education means for the deaf, absolute deprivation of the knowledge of the good news, of God, Christ and the Church. Therefore everybody, who has responsibility for the preaching of the good news, must be convinced that deaf people need education; that deaf children must get the opportunity to go to school.

The ideal situation for Catholic religious education of deaf children is the Catholic school, because religious education has to be integrated into the whole education; therefore schools should not be satisfied with half measures; they must be schools with a high standard of education.

We are aware of the fact that the situation is different in various countries. In many countries Catholic Schools cannot be realized or not in a sufficient number. In this situation the Catholic Church must see the special problem of religious education of the deaf and try to come into contact with the schools, especially with the Boards and Directors of these schools to give them help with respect to religious education.

RESOLUTIONS

1. We must educate the hearing people to a better understanding of the problems of the deaf.
   a. Visitors to schools for the deaf should be encouraged to spread interest in the deaf.
   b. Students in Seminaries and Teachers' Training Colleges should be invited to visit schools for the deaf.
   c. Teachers and others who work with the deaf should give lec-

tures at Universities particularly to Social Science students.

2. An appeal should be made to the Catholic Conference of Bishops of various countries for more attention to the deaf and their spiritual and educational needs.

3. At the Bishops' Conference one Bishop should be involved in the spiritual welfare of the deaf.

4. At least one professionally trained priest should be appointed, full-time where necessary, to look after the spiritual needs of the deaf in each diocese.

5. Irrespective of the general pastoral standards in a diocese, the needs of the deaf, must be seen as a continuing missionary need.

6. The handicap of deafness as distinct from other forms of physical and mental handicaps, requires special consideration and help. This need can only be met when the Bishop is both informed and involved.

7. The attention of Heads of Religious Orders should be drawn to the needs of special education for the deaf.

8. In schools run by religious, the participation of lay staff in organisation should be encouraged.

9. Every teacher has a contribution to make to the religious education of his pupils. The married teacher has much to contribute due to his experience of raising a family.

10. Catholic schools for the deaf and desirable with mixed staff. e.g. Nuns and/or Brothers teaching in 'lay' schools.

11. House mothers and 'out of classroom' staff in residential schools need special training in religious formation for their work.

12. In view of the great need for help for the Catechists who teach in other than Catholic schools, could time and money be provided to enable Catholic teachers to prepare materials suitable for use by these Catechists in their particularly difficult situation?

13. Research should be done on authentic Christian attitudes of deaf children. In this respect we need development of standardised texts and a set-up of exchangeable codes.

14. An information service on religious education of the deaf would be useful. e.g. a bulletin, a question-answer section for solutions to problems.

15. Exchange of thought between Catechetical centres on parent guidance in religious formation of deaf preschool children would be very helpful.

16. The Church's responsibility towards the deaf does not end with its responsibility towards the deaf who are Catholic, but extends

to the deaf who are not of our belief, or have no intention to share it and most likely even never will share it; for they too are in need; material and spiritual need, they too may have the divine gift of faith which needs activation.

17. We recommend the ordination of deaf, well-educated and suitably trained married men to the Deaconate.

18. Because of the complex and all pervasive nature, and isolation of deafness, the conference recommends that special consideration be given to the needs of the deaf for liturgical participation.

19. A second International Catholic conference should be held in the next future.

J. van Eijndhoven,
Chairman

Fundamental problems

1. Responsibility of the church to the deaf

P. Birch

The religious formation of the deaf raises many questions. The first of these, both in time and in importance, is that we need to be clear whether we are talking of the whole work of formation, or merely of formal instruction in religion. We need to be clear whether we are talking of formation in school, or formation in the community as a whole. We need to be clear that there are means of receiving formation besides hearing, and that deaf people have a right to these.

I suppose the first thing to disentangle is the purpose for which we give religious formation. It is to enable the person to lead a life of sanctity, a life of faith and hope and charity. He must be motivated to accept this way of sanctity with its values and its attitudes, and for this purpose he must be able to appreciate and understand it. The purpose is to make saints, not theologians, and it is to make saints now, not saints sometime in the future. It is important that this be understood, for it is possible that in our formation of the young we have placed too much emphasis on grown-up intellectual understanding. By doing so we may have made it cold and unattractive. We may have been too anxious about knowing with the mind, and not have made enough allowance for understanding with the heart, with affection and love. We may not have enabled our young people to realise that our faith is a matter basically of loving and of showing love. Therefore, Christ's new commandment is still a new commandment to many of his followers, to love one another as Christ loved is not how we would identify Christians. (Jn. 13.35). It is still a new unusual thought that God is love, (Jn. 4:16) and very few would describe God in this way.

Perhaps this brings me to the first step in my thinking about the religious formation of the deaf. Deprivation of hearing, like deprivation of sight, may, and probably does cause excessive introspection. The totally deaf person, like the totally blind, may turn in on himself too much, and may try to become completely self-sufficient. He can hardly avoid becoming an egocentric. He is not the only one, of course, who may suffer in this way, but it affects him more, I think. So we must try to bring him out, to attract him to others, (if necessary even to ourselves), and through them to God.

✝ To me, the really essential element in our religion is its community nature, and this is very often forgotten. We are people: we are God's people, with our individual abilities, resources and customs. No one can be in faith outside that people; no one can set himself apart from it and survive spiritually, much less grow, expand and blossom. Excessive individualism is impossible then: all sin has an anti-community element, for the sinner is setting himself and his own desires above the needs of others. To unity and harmony all our spiritual development must tend.

It requires great generosity, and sometimes a total spirit of sacrifice of oneself to be available to others to the extent that this requires. Only here, though, do matters like dedicated virginity and celibacy begin to make real sense. If we are God's people individuals among us must sacrifice our own needs for the sake of others. It is hardly an accident that Irish tradition called the completely trusting, unambitious, sexless simpleton a person of God's, a 'duine le Dia'. The whole paradox of faith and God's choice of mere children instead of the learned and clever, his use of these as stumbling blocks to pull us back to our senses is tied up in this idea of the foolishness of the Gospel.

It is, therefore, vitally important that, even more than other people, the deaf have proper personal experiences of religion. As far as possible these must be such as make it attractive, something the person will want. I have a vague notion of some of the difficulties involved in getting a deaf child to understand words and ideas. I am not rash enough to touch on this subject, except to repeat that we have tended to make the whole process of religious teaching too much a matter of words and ideas and thinking. The thinking has been too abstract and remote, and far from likely to win anyone to it. This is true of all our teaching, and not merely our teaching of the deaf. We have set a vast gulf between our theory, or our theories, and the practice of day-to-day living, loving God and loving people we live with. And we have forgotten that we cannot love God unless we love people, and unless people love us. It is in this way that formation is essential.

For the deaf and their formation this notion of loving is very important. It is both difficulty and an advantage. It is a difficulty that presents a great challenge when we consider that severely deaf people are liable to poor interpersonal relationships, to emotional under-development, to this egocentricity of which I spoke, and so may not be

4

naturally likely to form easy community relationships. It is a difficulty that deaf people tend to be introspective instead of outgoing. Possibly the same difficulty arises basically with many hearers, too, in this connection, but that is another matter.

But besides being a disadvantage, the community nature of real religion is an advantage towards formation. The deaf, and especially congenitally deaf, suffer from underdevelopment in conceptual formation. We allow ourselves to be far too discouraged by this thought. We tend to be pessimistic about their ability to comprehend and manipulate what are difficult abstract ideas for any one. The fact is that we have over emphasised this aspect of our faith for all, and not merely for deaf people. We have limited our instruction to the formulating of truths. We would be much nearer to arriving at the reality of a People of God if we accepted the fact that these concepts are difficult for many others besides deaf people, and because they are so difficult they cannot be completely obligatory.

We can be close to God without comprehending all these Pauline or scholastic concepts. They gave trouble right from the beginning. It is clear from the letters of St. Peter that his people were bothered by them. Indeed, St. Peter himself had problems in this field. He was an honest, affectionate man. He was ready to admit that Paul wrote with great wisdom, and wisdom which was Paul's special gift, in a way he himself could never do. 'He always wrote like this', Peter said, and then with a modesty that is endearing even today, he added, 'and this makes some points in his letter hard to understand'. Students and writers ever since have agreed, but not always with the same simplicity. This is not anti-intellectual or anti-inspirational. Christ had to open the minds of his disciples so that they could understand. (Lk. 24.45) St. Peter writes on a homely and easy plane to his disciples: 'You are new born and, like babies, you should be hungry for nothing but milk – the spiritual honesty which will help you to grow up to salvation'. Almost immediately, however, he breaks into the sublime lyrical passage which is far removed from simplicity: 'You are a chosen race, a royal priesthood, a consecrated nation, a people set apart to sing the praises of God who called you out of darkness into his wonderful light'. (1 Peter 2) The simple and the sublime are not far apart in the case of one who loves God.

We can leave that one, and take up another matter. I think we must advert to the place that gesture can and should play in the formation of the deaf, no matter what their condition. First of all, there is the comprehensive Christian gesture which has always been effective, which

5

is essential for all. It is the sign, the indication of love, and this sign has to be based on reality. It was this that attracted people to Christianity from the beginning. I think this love must have been particularly attractive to the underprivileged of Christ's time.

The first Christians had not much to impress their contemporaries with but this love of theirs for one another. It was enough. How they loved one another was a marvel at the time, not how they convinced and not how they explained or theorized. That was the test our Saviour offered – by this love we would demonstrate we were Christians. By this the value of our lives would ultimately be assayed. When he declared his policy at the beginning of his campaign, his policy was a revolution, and his care, his concern for sufferers were the main factors in his revoluion. At the end he prayed for his disciples that they would all be one with him, and by this fact, this gesture, this sign of an underlying reality, the world would be brought to believe that Christ was sent as the Son by the Father, that he was in fact a Person of the Blessed Trinity.

This is the over-all, the one absolutely vital, Christian gesture; it is the evidence of the lives that we lead. Without this there can be little real formation of anyone. Within this one gesture there are others that could and should be used to communicate with those who cannot hear, just as there are gestures to communicate with those who cannot see. But I think they must be real and meaningful in our lives. They would, in fact, help the religious formation of any of us.

Wordsworth was impressed and edified by the sight of a 'nun silent in adoration', even if the life of the consecrated religious woman probably meant little to him. So, too, we could learn and use the significance of certain basic postures and gestures. Some of these our Saviour himself used – we can raise our eyes and our arms to the Father, for example, as he often did. We can offer our hands to Christ and his Mother to lead us; we can lower our eyes and join our hands to listen to him in prayer, and be willing to be changed by him; and we can open our arms wide to draw all others to ourselves and to Christ, and let ourselves go with them. We can hold our heads high because, as Christians, we have a right to be proud of Christ, our brother.

I do not think that either the broad comprehensive gesture, the witness of our lives, or these lesser gestures, which indicate and teach a religious lesson, can be acquired or used merely for a purpose or an occasion. They must be a real natural part of our lives. Their meaning must be obvious to ourselves: this is very important. I think the gestures must be understood and intended by ourselves before we gon on

6

to try and get others to understand them too. There is an interesting and valuable principle here – the one who would wish to be able and effective as a teacher must accept a personal discipline which will make his effectiveness possible.

What is important then is to remain an individual, and at the same time to be assimilated into a society where faith and hope and love are realities, as I have been insisting it is. In this way real religion is taught. It is the best formation. It will be better done if the forming community is conscious of its forming power and works at it. Of all communities, the first and most effective educative community is, of course, the family. We should not forget this.

The members of a family may very well feel themselves inadequate to provide for the deaf child however hard they try, so great emphasis must be laid on helping the deaf person's family to do the work which it was intended to do. This does not detract from the specialist provision which the school alone can give. In fact, we know both from experience and from specialised studies, that this specialist provision is more effective where home teaching has preceded school, even residential school, and where during and after school parents are themselves introduced to the aids and methods that are used in the teaching of the deaf, and taught to have some understanding of them.

This family teaching and this learning by experience may be the ideal position, though it may not always be the fact. Deaf children must be formally taught. They must be taught because people expect it: the deaf will be thought to be uneducated if they cannot express themselves and explain their religious beliefs, no matter how well they live their faith. In this situation the deaf may suffer because they will think themselves badly done by. They must be taught for their own fulfilment, too, for reading, for thinking. They must be taught because they have to be in a special school and be separated from their families for other subjects, and so the family type of formation will be out.

Difficulty in communicating concepts still remains, however, as a real problem. It is a great problem for the deaf, with any deaf, and it is even more difficult if we try to cater for groups, for people whose deafness is due to different causes, cerebral palsy, or brain damage, for example. All deaf people simply cannot be treated in the same way, even if they are all profoundly deaf, or even if they are all only partially deaf. Whether the person has heard at any time will obviously make a differentiating factor too. It is simply not possible to separate the deaf on these refined bases, however, and yet group teaching or class teaching can be only partially recommended. The young deaf person must learn that it is religiously vital to belong to a group, and, paradoxically, group teaching for him cannot be depended on. It would seem that individual teaching becomes essential, therefore, and this must be our eventual aim.

Qualified teachers of religion for the deaf are a necessity. Providing such teachers in schools is not a problem in Ireland, fortunately. It can be assumed that deaf children will be in special schools. Special schools are staffed by qualified teachers of the deaf whose profession it is to communicate with children. These teachers are also instructed and informed practising Christians qualified in that field. We do not then have the problem experienced in other countries, that of getting a priest to give instruction. The only difficulty may be in the type of instruction; public opinion may demand this too conceptualised type of formation which I have been opposing.

Difficulties may arise, however, with partially deaf children who are being assisted, but are not in special schools. These may be gathered into classes for hard of hearing children, or they may be trying with hearing aids to get along in ordinary classes. Circumstances may force a partly qualified teacher of the deaf to staff these classes. For normal adult religious formation they will almost certainly have to depend on the priest in the parish. There is no doubt about the need for special training and support for teachers and parents in this situation. Both teachers and parents should be given help to cope with their situation, and, if at all possible, they should be led to help with other deaf people, and put theit training at the disposal of them.

Deaf people obviously need special care. It may be argued that like other handicapped people they should take their place in normal society. This is not always possible, and even if it were, I do not believe that everyone would think it desirable. A special chaplain or spiritual director of the deaf is desirable to cater for their needs. When this is mentioned, I find that a priest always comes to mind. This need not be so. A priest should be able to act through qualified people; the role of religious in formation, and the doctrine of the priesthood of the laity should be explored to this end. Sisters who have trained should be capable of the direct communication.

In this connection I may say that I am becoming more and more convinced that the work of priests, brothers and sisters is not to be found in the clearly defined, brightly lit places, such as schools and clinics, but in the grey areas of life, such as uncatered for areas of special need which are not popularly recognised. In many of those

8

areas it is difficult to find or retain people with special skills: deafness in the community is one of these. The sister or brother should be here, I believe; he or she makes continuity more likely, and this is important. More important is the fact that they show in a practical way the Christian attitude to concern for suffering and privation.

A special and separate problem that appears to come up in this regard is the psychological development of the deaf, or partially deaf adolescent. Adolescents want to be like others, not to be different. There may be natural resentment there when the young deaf person comes to realise, or is made to realise he or she is different because of his or her handicap. Peers may be unconsciously cruel too. This resentment may exacerbate the normal tendency of young people to reject and rebel. The young deaf person may be expected to lean naturally to introspection; too easily this introspection may become resentment and brooding. Here a knowledge of the psychology of the young is vital: so too is the ability to sympathise with the hopes of the young. Later on this ability may be needed even more when the same young person realises that normal married life is less likely for a deaf person than for others. In this regard, I might say in passing, that we could rethink our whole attitude to divine vocation. If we did, perhaps we might be better able to see that in the Christian way of thought, their affliction is not to be a sign of God's disfavour. On the contrary, it can and should be used for God, and God can make happy use of it.

Here perhaps we could mention something else that is of help. We ignore the vital virtue of hope in all this debate, and debates like it. I think we make three false assumptions. The first is that we assume that faith comes only from hearing. I have been trying to insist that faith comes from seeing, from copying, from all forms of personal communications. The second is that we seem to assume that faith comes independently of hope and charity. Possibly we accept charity as essential, too, but we seem to ignore hope completely. This is part of our pride. I think we are unconsciously inclined to depend on our own powers, rather than have confidence, assurance, conviction that God supplies what is spiritually necessary for us. There is a vocation to hope, a vocation we are called to.

We make a third mistake, too. We tend to limit hope to ourselves. We have whittled hope down into something that we wish for, but do not really expect. We forget that real hope is strong and urgent and is a community virtue, developed in community and found in community. We forget that it is linked with joy. It is at its best in those times when the natural resources we depend on have been taken from us, and we

9

are forced to depend on God and God's agents. The deaf, I think, come to terms with this condition more easily, and they could teach us a lesson here. They can teach hope. Hope is not less important than faith, and cannot, in fact, be separated from it. If we had real hope we would have faith; it would be a marvellous boost to a deaf person's morale if we could be seen to learn from him.

Like all other teaching, working with the deaf requires a great amount of personal maturity in the teachers. We must be able to accept things as they are, recognise what is possible, and what cannot be expected. The individual must be treated as a person who has a contribution to make community when his own personality has been developed. It rejects the application of hard uniform standards.

Pope Paul asks for a 'fierce regard for human dignity' in our relations with others. This is vital in teaching. In teaching the handicapped it is essential. One who prizes human dignity highly, fiercely, will not be condescending, will not be patronising with any handicapped person. We must love the handicapped, we must give them courage and hope – like all teachers, our aim is to make them independent of us, arrive at the stage when they will not need us.

I have met many young people recently seeking experience of religion in service of the handicapped. I have found them doing so in places where the basic philosophy seemed to be one that made the handicapped or the afflicted signs of God's harshness. Christ's attitude was not such, and a Christian's must not be so. Christ, as I said, made the service of suffering basic. St. Paul discovered that consolation for suffering derives from the risen Christ and overcoming all death and promising this to his followers. Young people would gladly respond to this if it was explained to them, and was seen being put into practice as you teachers of the deaf are doing in your lives.

QUESTIONS AND ANSWERS

Question
Your Excellency very properly put the *right* of deaf children on 'receiving formation'. Could you briefly detail that right and its sources, because this is a basic point in our work.

Answer
The right of deaf children to receive formation derives from:
a. The fact that a deaf child is a person and needs religious formation

to develop his personality fully. Because he is physically defective he may even have a claim in equity to have his defect compensated for.

b. The fact that he is a member of society gives him the right to be developed so that he can play a full part in social life. If his religious formation is defective he cannot play his full part.

c. The fact that he is a Christian, from the first Christian writings to the latest, as, for example, in Col. I 21-23, or as in the latest Papal Document, the Letter to Cardinal Roy: 'to defend their place and dignity in a society hardened by competition and the attraction of success'.

Question
You rightly put emphasis on the 'significance of basic postures' and you say: 'I think the gestures must be understood and intended by ourselves before we try to get others to understand them too'. Do you think that these gestures are *directly* meaningful by themselves, or only on a basis of language, especially because of the figurative meaning? e.g. a deaf child will not understand what the proper meaning of 'shaking hands' is unless he feels what is real friendship – without that it remains pure imitation. Would you say that the understanding of figurative meanings in religious education is of primary importance?

Answer
I think the gestures must spring from an inner meaning, i.e., be sincere – if a handclasp is cold a sensitive child will sense it, if, on the other hand it is not given, the handicapped person may not be aware of the existence of the emotion. Some gestures are directly meaningful, an embrace, for example, but, I think, in the context of a particular culture.

Question
You mentioned very important and basic convictions, as 'family teaching ... may it be the ideal position' and 'individual teaching becomes essential'. Could you define these views, especially in respect of their consequences to the acqiusition of classes and dormitories for deaf children?

Answer
I see teaching as one person working with another, each reacting to the personality of the other. In these circumstances it is ideally done

by individuals with individuals. Class teaching was a poor invention to make popular teaching possible because it would be cheap.

The family knows the child best, and particularly the handicapped one – where-ever possible the family must teach him, and where necessary be given the appropriate expertise.

No child can develop properly if it is considered part of a group, and least of all a handicapped one. The family can best cater for the child's individual and social needs at the same time. Every resource must be placed at its disposal, therefore, and the family has the right to expect this.

Question
You rightly oppose a 'too conceptualised type of formation' of children and of teachers too, especially in religious formation. Could you briefly explain your view in respect of the *content* of faith, because faith is not only an attitude, it also has content.

Answer
I think that faith must, of course, be explained, but before that both in time and importance the child (and the adult) must be introduced to its practice. This, the schools have not done. The most important element in its practice is love of God and of our neighbour. To date this has been no more than a sentence in the instruction of children.

12

2. Fundamental theological aspects of the special situation of the deaf in the church

J. Cahill

The most fundamental consideration of the Christian life will view it at the level of divine faith, since this virtue is at the very root of all Christian activity. Charity, for all its excellence, will ultimately depend on faith as will all liturgical worship and sanctification. Fundamental aspects of deaf people in the Church will mainly concern the activity of divine faith overcoming the handicap of deafness. If believing, normally comes through hearing, what is the peculiar situation of those burdened with deafness?

There are a number of very specialised fields in which this problem could be considered, e.g. the pedagogical, psychological or catechetical. I intend to proceed from the purely theological point of view, hoping that experts in those other areas will help out with criticism and suggestions.

To the best of my knowledge, a theology of the special situation of the handicapped, especially the deaf, has never been worked out. One consults the classical sources of theology in vain for any consideration of the problem. Consequently, it seems that the best way to proceed is to treat of the normal development of faith among the non-handicapped and then, in the light of this, evaluate the special obstacle of deafness.

The Catholic faith tells us that at Baptism the Christian becomes the temple of the Holy Spirit and that the gift of grace, which is a partici- pation of God's own life, is given to the soul. Life by its very nature is meant to grow and for this reason God gives the power of growth along with the new life, i.e. the Christian virtues of faith, hope and charity. The theological tradition of the Church has always distinguish- ed these virtues from grace itself and regarded them as supernatural operative powers related to grace more or less as the intellect and will are related to the human soul. It is through these virtues that grace becomes dynamic and the Christian, already reborn in Christ, actually lives the new life and grows up in Christ by performing Christlike actions. The full patrimony of Baptism, therefore, is seen at three different levels:

a. the indwelling of the Holy Spirit who will help in the performance of the future activities of the Christian life,
b. sanctifying grace, distinct from the Holy Spirit and virtues, which elevates the soul to a participation of divine life, and
c. infused virtues of faith, hope and charity through which the new life operates and manifests itself.

The theological virtues of faith, hope and charity must not be thought of as disembodied powers which somehow operate in a vacuum, independently of the human faculties of intellect and will. Believing, hoping and loving are vital conscious acts in which the human intellect and will are involved. The theological virtues are rather supernatural reinforcements of these faculties, elevating them to perform activities beyond the normal ambit. Until such time as the baptised Christian is capable of acting consciously, these basic Christian virtues are dormant. They are present but incapable of expression because of the lack of development of the human powers of mind and will in which they reside.

The aim of Christian educations is to activate divine faith as soon as possible, i.e. to bring about an actual conscious Christian belief. Only when faith is thus activated can Christian living begin. The exercise of hope and love is impossible without an active faith.

When exactly does the Christian life begin to operate in the normal unhandicapped child who has the benefit of an early Christian education? In other words, in ordinary circumstances when do the Christian virtues cease being dormant and really find expression in human activity? We may also ask what percisely is the influence of a teacher of Christian doctrine in activating the supernatural virtue of faith. It is only against the beackground of the answers to these questions that we can consider the handicap of deafness.

The act of faith is a peculiar mixture of the natural and supernatural, of sense experience and the transcendent. Essentially it is a *judgment* of intellect which is fortified by the supernatural virtue and immediately activated by the Holy Spirit. But for all its supernatural nature and origin, this same judgment involves earthly images which are the result of sense experience, and natural concepts which are expressed in words. It is only in the natural furnishing of human ideas and concepts that the deaf are handicapped in respect of divine faith. The intellect is already equipped with the reinforcing virtue, the Holy Spirit is already indwelling. Because of this Baptismal patrimony the deaf are less handicapped in respect of faith than they are with regard

14

to acquiring the natural sciences for which there is no such supernatural abiding help.

An example of the judgment of faith is the proposition 'Christ is our Saviour'. The supernatural element of this judgment is expressed in the verb 'is', whereas the ideas of 'Christ' and 'Saviour' depend on sense experience and purely human concepts. The role of the Christian educator is not to produce the vital affirmation 'is' in the act of faith. Only the Holy Spirit helps in this intimate region of the mind and wlil. Rather, the role of the teacher is to furnish the necessary concepts which will be joined by the act of faith when it expresses itself in judgment.

Further analysis of the act of faith will show another dimension of its transcendent supernatural character, that is, the motivation involved. The proposition 'Christ is our Saviour' could be made in all sincerity at a purely natural level and yet not be an act of divine faith. This would be so if the word 'Christ' merely signified a good man who lived in the past and who did good for humanity at large. The motivation for such a judgment would be merely human historical evidence, or at least the common acceptance of this fact. But the motivation of divine faith is not any human evidence, rather Divine Witness, divine authority. The intrinsic evidence for the judgment of faith is not apparent, and yet the mind assents because God, the Supreme Truth has said so. It is this motivation of divine witness given in revelation which radically distinguishes supernatural faith from mere human belief. When the Apostle said that faith comes by hearing, he was insisting on the role played by witness in this assent. Hearing is distinguished from seeing in so far as the latter involves immediate evidence for the judgment we make. A witness is heard, and what he tells may be accepted as true if we sufficiently appreciate his honesty. In the supernatural act of faith the ultimate witness is God Himself, even though He may use the witness of the Church, parents and teachers as his instruments in bringing his testimony to the individual soul.

So far we have considered two supernatural movements in the exercise of divine faith, and both of them under the immediate inspiration of the Holy Spirit. Firstly, there is the judgment of faith expressed in the verb 'is', such as 'God is merciful' and secondly, the acceptance of divine witness. It will be appreciated immediately that what we have described as the second movement is in fact the first and by far the more important. All judgments of faith presuppose assent to Divine Witness, i.e. that Divine Truth has spoken and is to be believed. It must be stressed again that these two movements are a special gift of God,

15

transcending all merely human persuasion, and are brought about by the immediate help of the Holy Spirit.

But now to return to the natural side of faith where the handicap of deafness intrudes. Human images, concepts and words are involved in so far as the divine message is clothed in these. Perhaps it would be well here to elucidate the role of these concepts and words in divine revelation in order to see more clearly the difficulty of the deaf. The earthly concept and word has an important function in the activation of the dormant virtue of faith, but at the same time this human element must not be exaggerated. Actual belief is the immediate gift of the Holy Spirit: dispositions for that belief come from human instruction.

When God revealed Himself to man, He used human ideas and words which have origin in sense experience, and ultimately in the material world around us. Of themselves, these words are infinitely below the divine wisdom which God wished to communicate. They are incapable of adequately representing a supernatural knowledge which is connatural to God alone. Yet God did use these words in conveying. His transcendent message and this fact alone is our guarantee that they are correct *as far as they go*. They are the human words and concepts of God's choice. Instruction, which is the prerequisite to the act of faith is concerned mainly with these ideas and corresponding words. The interior illumination of the mind of the believer comes from the Holy Spirit and in virtue of this, assent is given to a proposition of faith on the motivation of divine testimony. But the vital interior act, for all the divine help, still needs the ideas and words of nature. For the deaf, these concepts are slow in formulation, and even when they are laboriously communicated by signs and images, these same ideas will never have full effective use without the corresponding words, i.e. without language.

The most fundamental human idea which is necessary for the exercise of divine faith is the notion of God. Basically, assent to the unseen is given *because God has said so*. Without this ultimate motivation there is no act of faith. Certainly, God uses the witness of the Church, the ministers of the Church, parents and teachers to bring the Good News of Salvation. But, as already stated, these are mere instruments in the process of belief. Unless the Christian goes beyond all these authorities and subordinate witnesses and grasps the witness of God Himself, belief remains merely natural with no activation of the supernatural virtue of faith which is part of the patrimony of Baptism. Only by the help of the Holy Spirit is this ultimate authority of God grasped. It is a supernatural happening and the first great step in the exercise of divine faith, and yet it requires a natural predisposition, some notion of God. It is the first task of the Catholic teacher to build up this notion of the Supreme Being, the ultimate truth which has spoken to humanity, which cannot deceive nor be deceived.

In the case of the normal child, when exactly does faith become awakened? Is it not possible for even the non-handicapped child to have a mere natural belief in the story of Jesus, believing merely because parents or teachers have said so. For some time this must be the case, until an adequate notion of God is achieved. This notion when adequately built up through instruction will be used by the Holy Spirit to help the believer to adhere supernaturally to the authority of God. This consideration is not purely academic. Much depends on the earliest notions used in Christian education. The essential ideas must be singled out because the activity of faith depends on them, as will the exercise of the Christian life of hope and love.

To get some idea of God across to any child who has but recently reached the age of reason has its own inherent difficulties. How can such a notion be communicated to a child who is deaf? In this area, theology as such applies no answers. This is the specialised field of the psychologist, the catechist and especially those who have experience in teaching deaf children. Here reference must be made to a paper recently given by Fr. A. van Uden at St. Michielsgestel, Holland on 'How to teach a right concept of God to deaf children'. I had the privilege of attending this lecture and the following are some points made by the eminent author which struck me forcefully.

Fr. Van Uden stressed the importance and indeed the delicacy of getting this initial notion of God across to deaf children. With particular reference to the deaf, it is not a mere question of an image or an idea, but also of a subconscious attitude which depends on the child's very early educational experiences. The author stressed the necessity of a happy parent-child and teacher-child relationship. Such experiences are more relevant than usual in teaching a notion of God to a child who is deaf. Fr. Van Uden sets out a programme for building up the notion of God covering the years of primary schools and even beyond that. One notices how he makes use of all the biblical imagery, the original words and ideas which God used to reveal Himself to man. The author spoke of the obstacle of egocentricity which could be more prevalent in deaf children, living as they do in their world of silence, and he stressed the special necessity here of reinforcing moral attitudes to go hand in hand with religious instruction. He advises that all new ideas about God should be used immediately in prayers, thus linking faith with the religious affective life of the child. Towards the end of the paper Fr. Van Uden outlined a rational approach to the proofs of the existence of God for senior deaf children. It is hoped that in the near future Fr. van Uden's paper will be published, because it is obviously the product of deep scientific research and, equally important, experience.

Presupposing this first step in active faith which is the readiness to accept what God has actually testified, the message of revelation must be taught. In this message God has spoken about Himself in His own inner life, about His Son and about His Church. Catholic theology has considered the gradual acceptance of this message as a progressive set of judgments made with the aid of the Holy Spirit. All along this path of learning the deaf are handicapped in acquiring the new ideas which are part of God's message. And it seems that the handicap is not limited to the formulation of the concept, but even makes its presence felt in the use of that same concept in judgment. It is interesting to note that St. Thomas Aquinas in his rational psychology, sees a very intimate liaison between sense experience and the intellectual act of judgment. This dependence, according to St. Thomas, is not merely in the build-up towards judgment but even in the actual exercise of this vital act. Every judgment not only comes from sense experience but goes back to that same experience when it asserts that A is B. This process Aquinas calls 'resolution to sense experience' and is absolutely necessary if the judgment, even the judgment of faith, is to be valid. If this observation of St. Thomas is true, we see the obstacle of deafness carried on beyond the realm of ideas to the act of judgment itself. The inadequacy of fundamental sense knowledge through the lack of hearing, will obtrude at the level of the senses and thus obstruct the memory, and cause similar difficulty at the intellectual level of apprehension (concept) and in the process of judgment. It would be interesting to compare this theory of Aquinas with the findings of applied psychology. All the devotion, love and technical skill of the Catholic teacher is needed to make up this deficiency. The giving of language, where possible, is surely the greatest natural help of all. The message of love and hope which has been revealed by God in Christ is a matter of urgency for the deaf. No time may be lost in bringing Christ into their conscious lives.

Of all the Christian virtues, charity undoubtedly holds the primacy. It is the virtue of generosity, forgetfulness of self, living for others and of sacrifice. Very important in the present context is that it fights egocentricity which can so easily blossom in the silent world of the

18

deaf. That charity should find an outlet as soon as possible is imperative. Yet it is possible to over-emphasise the role of charity to the extent of minimising that of faith and the human concepts which are the furnishing of faith. Charity is helpless without an active faith. The mind must first of all appreciate in faith the infinite goodness of God, that He is loveable for His own sake and that all men are to be loved because they are children of God. But the goodness and love of God can only be appreciated in the life of Christ, in the words and deeds of Christ. In short, the absence of an active Christian faith makes the act of charity impossible. The technical language of theology which the Church has evolved over the centuries is not necessary to activate faith and consequently, the virtue of charity. For the deaf, such language would be a hindrance rather than a help. The words and imagery of the Bible are quite sufficient for this purpose. The inspired word of God will not fail to evoke faith and love. Initially, God revealed Himself by way of a salvation history in the Old and New Testament. This must be the most effective way of teaching faith to the deaf who would find it so difficult to assimilate the abstract terms evolved by the Church in her flight against heresy down through the centuries.

What has been said about charity holds also for the virtue of hope. Hope presupposes faith in the promises of God and the goodness and power of God to implement them. But this basis of hope is nowhere more apparent than in Christ, because nowhere does the power and goodness of God shine out more than in the Incarnate Word, in whom the original promises are revealed in their full sense. The normal source of hope and charity is Christian contemplation which is an exercise of faith. The life of Christ as depicted in the Gospels is the primary matter for that contemplation. Hence the necessity of inculcating a love of the Bible, especially the New Testament, in the deaf. If they are cut off from the audible voice of the Church, the Gospel takes on an even more significant role for them than for other Christians.

Not only is faith the foundation of hope and charity, it is the means of participating in the Christian liturgy which principally consists of the seven sacraments. Our sacraments are external sign-actions of faith which are built up by the Church and the faithful. They begin as external expressions of belief in the saving influence of Christ, and end with the actual accomplishment by Christ of what is signified. Here again the deaf are handicapped since most of these sign-actions involve language. Not that language is essential to the expression of our faith, but it is the most normal human means for this end. The Eucharist is the very centre of the liturgy and active involvement here, more than anywhere else, fosters the community dimension of our religion. Eucharistic liturgical action is most necessary for the deaf who might be apt to consider themselves aloof from the rest of the Christian community. The Eucharist is the sacrament of Christian unity, uniting the faithful with Christ and among themselves. To what extent is it possible to get the deaf involved in the normal parish Mass, I cannot say. Neither can I judge on the feasibility of having a separate Mass for the deaf in which they might participate more confidently.

So far I have endeavoured to give a theological analysis of faith as the foundation of the Christian life, and its activation through religious instruction with particular reference to the deaf. But now, presupposing religious instruction, we must look ahead and consider the evolution of that Christian life. Does deafness remain such an abstacle for the lifetime development of faith as it shows itself to be at the beginning? How does faith develop in the soul – does it become more complicated or more simple? The whole Christian tradition of ascetical and mystical theology answers that faith develops to maturity in simplification. Language and concepts become less and less important because mere human expression becomes less relevant to the insights afforded by the Holy Spirit as the Christian soul becomes more involved with God. The Church has always acknowledged the gifts of the Holy Spirit which help the Christian virtues in areas where ordinary language becomes insufficient. Through these gifts the Holy Spirit inspires, and the exercise of faith, hope and charity, as a result, is described as 'suprahuman': *modo supra humano*. In this progressive spiritual life, human concepts lose their importance. The action of the Holy Spirit is less tied up with what is merely human, and the corresponding insights and judgments of faith can hardly be expressed in words.

There is obviously a special Providence for the handicapped and we can see here in the realm of the gifts of the Holy Spirit how this Providence can act with reference to the deaf. What proves such an obstacle at the beginning, progressively diminishes as the Holy Spirit takes over the role of teacher, giving insights and consolations which cannot be described in mere human words.

To end this paper I should like to depart from these particular considerations and touch briefly on a broader aspect of the deaf in the Church. What I am about to say is occasioned by the fact that the documents of Vatican II, while having something to say about the poor, have nothing to say about the handicapped. When John the Baptist sent his disciples to ask Christ if he were the Messiah, the answer

20

of Christ was to tell John of what they had seen – Christ's preoccupation with the blind, the deaf and the handicapped in general. Indeed, this was the special sign given by Isaiah by which the Messiah would be recognised. This love for the underprivileged has always been reflected in the life of the Church. It is still here to-day and your presence at this Congress is witness of that. Yet we notice a new awareness of the handicapped in the modern welfare state, an awareness such as has never been manifested before. Now, more than ever, the love of the Church for the underprivilged must shine out.

To a certain extent, all Christians are handicapped, and all religious institutes involved in apostolic activity are somehow working for the underprivileged. But after the example of Christ special love must be shown to the mentally and physically retarded. I do not think that it would serve any real purpose here to ask all religious apostolic institutes to abandon their schools and hospitals and devote themselves exclusively to these. Other apostolic activities, built up with the labour of centuries, cannot be so easily abandoned, nor would the Church desire such a course of action. But surely it is possible for every religious institute in the Church to devote some of its personnel and resources to the handicapped, and not as a mere concession: rather, following the example of Christ, giving this work pride of place and priority of consideration.

QUESTIONS AND ANSWERS

Question
Is faith confined to a movement of the intellect or does it involve the will as well?

Answer
Faith means the adherence of the mind to a given truth without the intrinsic evidence. One believes because one *wishes* to believe. All believing and especially the act of supernatural faith involves the movement of the will. The initial act of faith involves the movement of the Holy Spirit helping both will and intellect. Subsequently the life of faith will be informed, i.e. enriched or enlivened by charity. Thus believing will always depend on loving – as will charity in a different way, depend on faith.

In my paper I have emphasised the intellectual aspect of faith since the virtue was considered from the pedagogical viewpoint. The element of 'heart' in faith has already been covered by Dr. Birch.

Question
You mentioned 'Supreme Truth' and 'divine authority' as motives for our faith. Cannot these expressions be conceived purely naturally?

Answer
In the context of divine faith the motivation is purely supernatural. It is a motivation which is grasped not by reason alone, but by the special help of the Holy Spirit. To bring out the transcendence of this motivation it would be better to say 'God our Father speaks' rather than the cold phrase 'Supreme Truth'.

Question
In your paper you state that the human words used by God in revelation are valid 'as far as they go'. Could you explain this further?

Answer
In faith, God has communicated divine knowledge to a human mind, and in the process has picked human words, in spite of their inadequacy. These words could not *possibly* fully represent *divine* transcendent truth. Yet, God used them and this is our *guarantee* that they point in the right direction, and at the *same time* we are aware of their limitation. These words, divinely chosen, will not mislead us. Rather, under the guidance of the Holy Spirit, they are the very best means to give our minds an inlet into God's message.

Question
You explained the act of faith as a judgment expressed with the copula 'is'. Is it necessary that these judgments of faith are always *consciously* expressed?

Answer
No! Such explicit formulation is not necessary for the exercise of divine faith. In fact, when faith develops to influence human life more and more under the inspiration of the gifts of the Holy Spirit, the individual progressively becomes less conscious of this activity.

22

Language and religious education

3. Teaching an oral mother-tongue to deaf children in reference to religious education

A. van Uden

INTRODUCTION: PRELINQUALLY DEAF CHILDREN, NOT MULTIPLY
HANDICAPPED

We will only speak about such children, who are truly prelingually deaf, i.e. with losses of more than 90 dB. present at least before their second birthday. Secondly, we will not make reference at the moment to multiply handicapped deaf children, especially not to deaf children with the emotional disturbance of the type to which I referred elsewhere as the 'desolation syndrome' (Van Uden, 1970). We limit our paper to the 'normal prelingually deaf children', because these multiple handicaps give rise to so many complications, that we cannot treat them here in one hour only.

I. THE GOAL TO WHICH WE AIM – AUTHENTIC CHRISTIANITY

We aim at an authentic Christianity in our deaf children and adults.

What is authentic Christianity? It is real love of our Father in heaven and universal love of all men, even our enemies, by the redemption of Christ.

What does redemption mean? In its negative respect: the liberation from our egoism (i.e. the conquest of the weakness of our 'flesh', Rom. 7.5). Concerning the deaf, Jesus himself has characterised their special redemption (if you like, their therapy) with one word: 'Effatha!' i.e. 'Open'. We may say: Education of the deaf is an education towards openness.

This view prevents all attempts at an 'indoctrination' (Wilson 1971). Indoctrination narrows the mind, limiting the freedom of choice by continuous one-sided propaganda and/or brainwashing. Religious education can deteriorate indeed to a kind of indoctrination, but the aim of a *universal* love is then missed immediately, and replaced by a love narrowed by resentment and anguish, as we see so often in these modern times. Even if this narrowed love brings men to sacrificing themselves totally, it is now the love of Christ. We have seen this in so many Germans for instance, who went into the fire for their local idol Hitler: this was just fanatical love narrowed by indoctrination. Real Christian faith, hope and love cannot be injected. They cannot be bought, nor imprinted. We can only realise the usually indispensable *conditions* for them, so that they can be evoked and stimulated by the grace of God.

Authentic Christianity in the deaf?

This authentic Christianity is possible in the deaf, notwithstanding specific difficulties. I think we have all met at least some deaf adults, who came to a state of real forgiveness, of openness to everybody, of humility and generosity in the love of Christ, which cannot be explained by a sociologic and conventional indoctrination. We however, should not underestimate the specific difficulties. Ch. M. de l'Epée already said that the deaf will never be more than mere 'copyists' ('des copistes' cf. Büchli 1948). Although he condemned his own method of education by saying so – there may be some truth in this assertion.

Naffin (1933) and Gregory (1938) found that the development of real friendship among the deaf was retarded by some years, and that more than hearing children they remained longer in a state of ego-centricity.

Gordon (1962) found, that deaf children had difficulties in delaying the immediate satisfaction of their needs, more than hearing children.

Kallman (1963, Rainer a.o. 2d. 1969) and Myklebust (1964) found retardations in the sexual identification process especially of male deaf adolescents and adults.

Nass (1964) found, that the moral judgement of deaf children was 2 to 3 years behind that of hearing children, in so far that they were inclined to judge the moral content of actions too one-sidedly according only to the external effects. A recent example: two months ago I posed this problem in a sermon to two groups of children 9-10 years of age. 'Peter you are very smart. You always get the highest marks in your class. You are also very helpful and kind. John, you are a little bit of a romper! But one day you have an accident. You break both of your legs. You become paralysed! You must stop swimming, stop playing soccer, you can no longer walk, you must be driven in a small car'. (All the children agreed that he was in a very bad way.)

26

'But nevertheless you are always very kind, very patient for instance even when once the BROTHER forgot to give you pudding. Who is now the best boy? Peter or John?' All children answered: 'Peter!'

Kates and Kates (1965) found, that the development of social concepts is hampered in deaf children.

Lewis (1968) found that deaf children were retarded in the understanding of 'orectic' words (i.e. words of feelings, desires and so on). He found a correlation between the knowledge of personal ethical words and the adjustment/maladjustment of deaf children's behaviour.

Sarlin and Altshuler (1968) found deaf adolescents to be more aggressive among themselves than their hearing peers.

Van Lieshout and IJsseldijk (1970) found that such deaf children who lived with other deaf people in one family from birth, were more aggressive than deaf children living in a hearing environment.

I think we all agree, that there is a special danger, that the deaf will never achieve a higher faith than that of conventionalism (i.e. by a kind of indoctrination), a believing only because they are educated that way, simply not seeing other possibilities, with the result that their faith becomes too much an external way of life, very dependent upon external actions and objects, but with insufficient conversion from a sometimes strong egoism. Added to these is the danger that they lose the faith as soon as these convictions are withdrawn.

Nevertheless we will not aim at just keeping our deaf 'sheep' together, but at an authentic Christianity of as many deaf people as possible.

II. TEACHING A MOTHER-TONGUE

Are there pre-conditions, which should be implied in order to achieve our aim of authentic Christianity, of real charity in as many deaf children and adults as possible? The main pre-disposition seems to be *conversation*. And here we are at the heart of the education of the deaf! We would set up 4 basic theses:
1. Without real conversation it will be impossible to educate a child, deaf or hearing, towards love and charity.
    Conversation implies:
    Exchange of thoughts (not just a play of questions and answers); co-partnership; not only speaking to each other, but more listening to each other i.e. accepting each other.

27

If for instance a father and/or mother do not listen to the child, they show they do not accept him for his own personal value. The consequence will be the dangerous 'desolation syndrome', which includes a lack of love, an always subconscious hunger for love, and alas, an inability to give love. (Kogan and Moss 1962, Stott 1966, Schmahlohr 1968, Kay 1970).

Conversation implies fellow-feeling, an entering into each others' thoughts, pulling oneself into the place of the other, to some extent 'losing one's soul in order to save it' (Mc. 8.35), because by fellow-feeling we come to ourselves and to 'insight'.

We conclude: A human being loves in the way he has conversed from his early years of life.

2. The mother-tongue is that language in which one converses most spontaneously. Therefore, if we do not teach deaf children in a conversational way in the classroom, the *mother-tongue* deaf children will acquire is a gibberish of signing, perhaps mixed up with some speech, in free-time.

3. That low standard gibberish used in their free-time, among children of low standard thinking and behaviour, will show an insufficient basis for development of charity, and will therefore hamper the outgrowth of authentic Christianity.

4. If we do not put a conversational teaching of our mother-tongue into the heart of our whole education of the deaf, we will fail in the Christian education of too many deaf children.

How can we put the conversational teaching of a mother-tongue into the heart of our education?

At this moment we will make abstraction of the type of language: it may be oral language, a graphic language, a finger-spelled language, a language in mouth-hand-system or even a sign language.

The secret of teaching a mother-tongue to deaf children is the playing of a double part and the 'seizing method' (Van Uden, 1968).

How do you enter into conversation with a small speechless and languageless child? This is not so strange a problem! Every mother has to solve that problem with each new baby, whether he can hear or not.

Many teachers of the deaf think, that the building up of a vocabulary is necessary as a first step. This assumption is not true. A mother of a hearing child does not start in this way. For instance the baby laughs at his mother and at the milk. This utterance is immediately 'seized' by the mother who says: 'Lovely milk! Do you like milk?

28

Come here, darling!' What is happening here? The mother 'seizes' the speechless utterance of the child and gives it back to him in its correct linguistic setting. At the same time she says what she herself wants to say: 'Come here, darling!' And the child is picked up. So she plays a double part:

She 'seizes' what the child cannot yet say but seemingly wants to say; she says it for him – and she says what she herself wants to say.

After a time the child will understand 'Come here, darling!' And after a time again he will call 'milk' or something like that. This develops into short conversations between mother and child, in which the mother continues to play that double part from the first through the sixth year in the life of the child.

An example (Van Uden, 1968):
The mother is peeling an orange for the father who is expected home in a few minutes.

Lacitia, 2 yrs. old:	*Mother:*
Mmm nice!	It is nice, it is for Daddy!
Nice Daddy!	Yes it is nice, it is for Daddy! Daddy likes oranges!
Daddy o'ange	Orange (pronounced very melodically)
O'ange (the same melody)	
O'ange!	Orange! How cute you can talk! You
O'ange!	must tell Daddy!
Daddy o'ange (very melodically)	
Daddy coming	
Car?	No, Daddy is not coming by car. He is taking the train.
Titia car, he?	No, not today, Sunday we are going in the car . . . Look here, the orange is ready.
Daddy o'ange!	
Daddy o'ange!	
Daddy o'ange!	
(Skips away)	

The same happens – in principle – with deaf children. We had several pairs of parents – among them three pairs of deaf parents – who succeeded in teaching their deaf child lipreading before his first birthday, by way of operant conditioning, the 'anticipatory way' (Van Uden, 1963). An example of a conversation with a born deaf boy – Peter, $2^1/_2$ years old. He could still only speak 'Brrr . . .' He used this 'Brrr . . .' for all his wishes, refusals, calls, confirmations, questions etc., but always with a clear difference in the expression of his face. Once he pointed to the refrigerator.

Peter:	Mother:
Brrr!	Do you want an ice-cream?
Brrr?	No, we are first going to have a bath! A bath!
	Yes, we are first going to have a bath,
Brrraa!	and after that you will have an ice-cream!

While he is in the bath he keeps saying 'Brrraaa!' . . . 'Brrraaa' . . . and the mother keeps echoing: 'Yes, a bath'. This 'brrraaa' was a new word for Peter, his second.

This 'seizing method' and 'playing a double part' is continued in our schools. Our whole method of teaching deaf children a mother-tongue is built on conversation, on the way a mother follows, guided by nature. The effect of this method is *anthropological*, so the child feels accepted. He feels that all his serious utterances, wants, judgements, ideas, questions and so on are worthwhile. He is accepted as a co-partner in the whole of his behaviour, which gives him a real basis for happiness.

Three points may be clear:
1. Our catechesis should be given in a conversational, a 'seizing' way. A form of catechesis by lecturing to the children seems to be fruit-less and a waste of time. The catechist should first of all evoke reactions from the children, listen to them and 'seize' what they are giving spontaneously.
2. Education of deaf children, i.e. an 'internalising' of a way of life, is inconceivable without conversation. The education of deaf children in a large group, with only a kind and quiet atmosphere and much opportunity to play, seems insufficient. The educator should first of all converse with his children, which mainly means let them speak themselves, listen to them and make them feel accepted in love.
3. Last but not least: our task is not finished in school and free-time. We emphasise the paramount importance of training the parents: our work is only finished when we have brought the deaf children into real conversation with their parents. We do not educate deaf children for themselves, nor for the deaf club, but for their parents.
This is the indispensable and primary aim of a real integration into a

hearing world. I think we build the Christianity of our children on sandy foundations, if we fail in this point.

III.   CATECHESIS AS A PROBLEM OF LANGUAGE AND LIFE

A job or hobby can be just a piece of our life, which can bear little relation to the other parts of life. Not so religion. True religion is something, or better 'Somebody' penetrating all parts of our life, in some way or other. This is the reason that mission-work cannot be limited to preaching and teaching of faith and baptism alone, but includes, at least in the beginning, the teaching of reading and writing, care for the sick etc., thus follows schools, hospitals, roads, bridges and so on, i.e. the opening of a primitive world of fears and rigidities and narrowness to a higher freedom, as a matrix of authentic Christianity. To me religious education of the deaf is mission-work and includes the whole child. If not, there is a great danger that their religious education remains just an external veneer with no redeeming penetration (Van Uden, 1963).

1. Which medium of conversation?

We repeat the two strings of interconnections: Conversation is in life and life is in conversation, i.e. language without conversation misses life.

Religion is in life and life is in religion. Therefore conversation is indispensable for religious education. This means, that we cannot properly educate deaf children religiously without using that medium of communication in which they converse spontaneously.

In order now to prevent any misunderstandings, I must first of all confess that I am a pure oralist, which means, that I am convinced that the monolinguistic oral way in school and free time is not only possible, but the best way of education for all normal deaf children and also for the majority of multiply handicapped deaf children.

But there are schools for the deaf, in which the main means of communication in free time among the children of 8-9 years of age themselves is not speech, but signing. It may be a use of signs invented by themselves, or perhaps a systematic sign-language composed by hearing people. This very often means that a smooth oral converastion is not possible. I think we all agree, that much language should be acquired before real catechesis can start. But should we force catechists

to use the pure oral way, if the children cannot converse this way ...
if this has failed? It should however not fail! It can be so well developed that spontaneous conversation in that way is possible. But in many
schools it has not been developed to such a high standard. Should we
blame catechists then for using the sign language of the children,
because the oral way appeared to have failed in that school? I think
that if catechesis cannot be given conversationally (of course by an
expert in teaching the deaf, Hourihan 1963) without signing, such a
school compells the catechists to use the signs of the children (cf.
Stoevesand 1957, Weber in Anon. 1968). If these are not used, there
is to me a big danger that our whole religious education remains something of the school, but not of their life. My reasoning is as follows:

> Catechesis should be given conversationally; therefore catechists
> should use those means of conversation in which the children are
> able to converse:
> If the children cannot converse smoothly without signing, the cate-
> chist is compelled to use that signing notwithstanding the whole
> philosophy of the school.

The school has failed in its task and should take the educational consequences.

Perhaps catechists can then reveal that failure and it may be that the
school will revise its way of working.

I would hope so.

Consequently I do not agree with some teachers (e.g. Maesse 1967),
who say that the catechesis should always be given purely orally. This
depends on the oral standard of the school. I do not agree with some
teachers (e.g. Sr. Bridget 1962, Tigges 1963) who will compel catechists to use a completely programmed language followed by the
school, which hampers the spontaneity of conversation too much. I do
not agree with those teachers (e.g. Bridget 1962, Maesse 1967, Winn-
wisser and Götzen in Anon. 1968), who use so many pictures in teaching religion, that it creates a kind of picture or iconic thinking in matters of religion, instead of really conversational thinking. But I agree
with these words: catechesis needs 'integration of everyday experiences
and appreciations' (Bridget 1962). This however is only possible by
using that means of conversation which the children are using themselves. Concerning pictures: the first pictures should be drawn by the
children *themselves* after or during the *conversational* lessons.

I repeat my basic thesis: religion should be something of life, not
just something of school.

2. Developing ideas outside catechesis but in service of catechesis: basic ideas expressed in language

God's revelation uses human words and therefore human ideas too. God cannot reveal Himself, at least not by the way He usually follows, to languageless infants or severely mentally retarded or uninstructed deaf. So a basis of language should be laid down before catechesis can start. More and more fundamentals of language should be laid down in the higher grades, on which the catechesis can be built. Which basic ideas, expressed in language are these?

It is impossible of course, to explain them all here, but I would like to give some of them, which seem to me very fundamental but difficult, so much so that they ask for special care. I would divide them into two types:

a. figurative meanings.
b. very abstract, nuanced meanings.

a. *Figurative meanings*

Some teachers (e.g. Breitinger 1968) think it is impossible to teach deaf children about figurative meanings. This is not true. Happily it is quite possible (in fact necessary too), if tried in the right way.

This should already be prepared in the preparatory school by the development of the make-believe play, the play of pretending. E.g. 'Peter is a cat', 'that block is my car', 'you play a fish' and so on.

The second step is, that words can have a 'double meaning' (do not be afraid to use that term!), which often is found by intelligent children themselves, e.g. a 'letter' for written phonems and for a message, a 'stop' for a bus and a stop at the end of a sentence, 'watch your watch!' etc. The children should be familiar with this not later than first grade.

In the second grade or earlier, the term 'figurative meaning' which properly cannot be missed, can be given first for very clear and trivial expressions such as: 'the car is *running*', 'the tap is *running*', 'the flowers are *sleeping*', 'the book which hurts you is *naughty*' and so on.

We should however at this stage prevent a big mistake: that the term 'figurative' includes 'unreality'. The opposite of 'figurative' is just 'literal', not 'real'. Something can have a figurative meaning and yet be very real, e.g. a wedding-feast. So if one asserts: 'The Ascension of Christ has a figurative meaning and *therefore* did not really happen', he displays much misunderstanding. The so called 'prophetic actions' as for instance that of Jes. 19.10, where the prophet broke a stone bottle in order to prophetise the dispersion of the Israelites, really happened and notwithstanding that, had figurative meaning.

These principles should be applied for instance to these terms:

Belief: and faith for both the act of believing and for its content; for both a conviction or persuasion and for a pure supposition. Some teachers (e.g. Breitinger 1968) think that we should avoid the term 'belief' because it is confusing due to its double meaning. They prefer to say for instance 'I *know* that Jesus is present' instead of 'I *believe* that Jesus is present'. This is based, in my opinion, on wrong assumptions concerning language acquisition.

Food for our nourishment, and wooden blocks feeding fire, or letters feeding love etc.

Spirit for a soul, a ghost, but for actuating emotions, for frame of mind too.

Sin for a moral shortcoming, but also in 'What a sin, what a pity, what a shame', etc.

Deliverance from a prison, but also from a difficulty, from slavery to alcohol, from slavery to egoism, etc.

Penetration of the rain through the thin coat, but also of salt into food, of light into darkness, of fire into iron, of grace into a person, of Omnipresence into the world, etc.
We should not forget the meanings of gestures, e.g. of greeting, of bowing, also liturgic gestures (Schulte 1966), the meanings of customs, e.g. the use of black cloths in solemnities, of giving flowers and presents, of doing the same in the name of another, of celebrating feasts etc., etc.

It may be clear that the understanding of all this is indispensable in order to open the meanings of the parables to our deaf.

b. *Abstract and nuanced meanings*
The term 'abstract' may be somewhat misleading, because many terms are not so much abstract as nuanced, concerning atmospheres and feelings. For instance, the ideas of humble subservience which is so central in Christian attitude: the idea of fidelity and loyalty as the Christian aspects of obedience; the idea of making amends, pardoning and for-

giving (including guilt, conscience, sorrow): the idea of idealism, of surrendering oneself, etc.

These ideas can already be taught from daily conversations *long before* catechesis starts, e.g. 'You are faithful'; 'Who will serve Mary?'; doing something 'on purpose' or 'by accident' (in connection with this, very soon the ideas of 'choosing' should be explained in such situations); 'You are responsible for that'; 'My conscience is clear'; 'Without meaning any harm'; 'Now you got out of bed on the right side'; 'Yes, Peter also wants to go out by car, but he is not jealous of you!' (many deaf children use the word 'jealous' mistakenly!); 'You are not reasonable'; 'Appearances are deceptive'; 'It is more apparent than real'; 'We will take things as they are'; 'Men are more easily lead than driven'; 'Charles had pleaded guilty'; 'That work is ideal'; 'You must search after the best'; and so on.

An important idea is that of human happiness. This can be prepared by using very often such expressions as: 'Thank goodness!' 'A good thing too!' 'How happy you are!' 'What a piece of luck!' All this in very many different circumstances makes the idea abstract.

Another important idea, is that of pure chance in contrast to necessity or determination. Our human existence is not by pure chance, nor is it a matter of course; it is a vocation, is it not? This can be prepared by such expressions as: 'It is more by hit than by wit', 'You were lucky to escape', 'It so happened that I found it', 'Of course!' 'That is a matter of course!' 'Naturally!' 'We cannot take that for granted'.

Again a very important idea is that of mystery. This idea should not be used one-sidedly negatively as e.g. 'the disappearance of your expensive watch is a mysterie', but more positively: e.g. at the birth of a new baby. 'What will happen in his later life?' or 'That baby is a miracle, is he not?' or 'The astronauts may find beautiful mysteries there', and so on.

3. Importance of Catholic Schools?

We would like to draw two conclusions:

a. Catechesis stimulates the language acquisition enormously, even in its preparations. Many ideas, of which we would not have thought, are suggested. It drives us out from a too schoolish teaching of knowledge to the wideness of life, to feelings, to abstractions, to real humanisation.

b. I think that all this presupposes a Catholic school for deaf children.

How can all these necessary and indispensable ideas be prepared by teachers, who are not sufficiently aware of them, who do not see their interconnections with higher Christian Life? I think that most of these ideas (I gave only a few examples) are usually insufficiently prepared in non-Catholic schools, with the consequence that catechesis cannot demonstrate to full advantage.

VI.   READING AND RELIGIOUS EDUCATION

We will first explain what reading is; then the possibilities for deaf children; and finally its connections with religious education.

1. What is Reading?

We distinguish three kinds of reading (Van Uden, 1969, 1971):

a. 'Ideovisual Reading'
This is the lowest degree of reading which begins in the preschool with children of 4¹/₂ years of age: The point is that *from* the conversations in the classroom the teacher composes a reading lesson, e.g.

For Children of 4 Years of Age
John has built a house.
Charles said: 'I will build a house too.'
John said: 'That is my house!'
There were two houses.
Mary wanted to put her doll in Charles's house.
Charles said: 'No!'
Mary was very sad.

For Children of 5 Years of Age
Peanuts.
What is this?
It is a pea-nut.
A handful of pea-nuts.
We are going to open the pea-nuts.
Ellen says: 'Bite the pea-nuts!'
'No!'
William says: 'Open it with a knife!'
'No! Break it by hand!'
Marc cannot do it.
William can do it.
Oh! The shell is empty!
Into the paperbin!

36

The children can read these lessons (see Van Uden, 1968, 1971). Then they read *what they already know*: they already have the ideas, and find them within the written forms, in a more or less undifferentiated way.

This is ideovisual reading. Some deaf children, as some hearing children, will never rise above this lowest level of reading.

b. *The second degree of reading is 'receptive reading'*
This means, that the child grasps some *new* ideas from the written forms. For instance a boy of 6 years of age understood from his mother's letter, that his father bought a new blue car. This is reading in its real sense, if it concerns *normal* language of normally hearing children but it develops through these two phases: reading in the vocabulary phase and reading in the structural phase.

aa. *'Reading in the Vocabulary Phase'*
The child knows almost all words and idioms of the reading piece and guesses more or less intelligently what should be the meaning of the whole and the parts. This early understanding is very important. Many of these children like to read and they read usually with success. The structure of language, however, still plays only a minor part. The latter develops in the Structural Phase.

bb. *'Reading in the Structural Phase'*
This is reading in the strictest sense. The child, in addition, mainly understands the structure of the language in the reading piece i.e. the right grouping of words, the meaning of the tenses, the flexions, hidden figurative meanings and so on. About 40 % of hearing children in normal primary schools (i.e. excluding handicapped children) reach this level in the 4th grade of the primary school, i.e. at about 10 years of age.

2. *Possibilities of Deaf Children*

We refer now only to the reading of books for normal children, i.e. with normal language, not books with constructed or programmed language.

The results of many researches in this respect are very dissatisfying. The research by Wrightstone and others (1962) confirmed by that of Gentile and others (1969) showed that only 6 % of the prelingually deaf children of 16 years of age, could read in the strictest sense of the word. About 30 % of them could not read perceptively at all. 64 % could read more or less by guessing, i.e. in the vocabulary phase.

Thank goodness we can show better figures.

All prelingually deaf children of 16 years of age:

	Structural Phase	Vocabulary Phase	Scores of only Ideovisual Reading
1968	46 %	43 %	11 %
1971	42 %	58 %	0 %

So we must conclude that at least 40 % of all deaf children (*including the multiply handicapped*) of 16 years of age are able to read in the strictest sense. When this level is not reached, there must be something wrong, in my opinion, perhaps due to the methods used, the training of teachers, or even the organisation of the school, especially in free time.

The figures mentioned above imply that about 60 % of all children of 16 years of age read the literature of normally hearing children, from simple books for children of 10-12 years of age, through (some of the grown-up) books of the 'belles-lettres'.

3. Importance of reading in reference to religious education

I propose three points: reading and humanisation; reading and the belonging to the Church; reading and the discrepancy between intelligence and achievement.

a.   The most important point is that, when deaf children are able to read, they humanise more and more. They enter the world of culture. They learn much more from the wisdom of life. Their understanding of life becomes richer and richer. Humanisation is basic, in my opinion, for a deeper Christianisation. There is a danger, of course, that they will also read what can harm them, but on the other hand, their personal initiative is stimulated; they can become Christians of their own accord, by their own choice. It depends on the educators to guide this richer initiative to true idealism.

b.   Another point, not less important than the first: these children can read many parts of the Holy Scripture in its original translation. They can read the original documents of the Church; the normal prayer-books; the hymns of the Church; and so on. If they cannot read them independently, they can be helped to understand the main part at least. Therefore, they are not so detached from their parents, brothers and sisters, from their community etc.

You know that in almost every country special catechisms, special prayer-books and so on (Tigges and Götzen 1952, Löwe and Lauerer 1960) are published for deaf children and deaf adults. If the children cannot read and – especially if the schools follow strictly programmed language methods there is a necessity to have special prayer-books. But there is another possible way. Not only do we always prefer that small children compose their prayers themselves, guided by their parents, their teachers and by their houseparents, but we follow a free language method, first of all aiming at a flexible understanding of normal language, perhaps in the beginning in an undifferentiated way. The consequence of this is, that even for the children who cannot (as yet) read, the normal prayers, and many parts of the Holy Scripture can be explained, so that there is no need for especially composed textbooks in programmed language. To me there is a big difference between deaf children educated by a programmed constructive method and those educated according to a free method with a lot of spontaneous conversation and reading of normal language. The difference seems to be so great, that I think we can speak of two different kinds of deaf children.

c. One of the most dangerous aspects seems to be the discrepancy between the intellectual level and the achievement level of the deaf. This can be expressed by the discrepancy of the performance IQ and the verbal IQ (e.g. by the Wechsler Intelligence Scales). The verbal IQ includes not only vocabulary and calculation, but also general knowledge, common sense and analogic thinking. We found in deaf children of 13 years of age and over, (including the multiply handicapped), an average of 12 $\pm$ 8 points.

Age (examples)	Performance I.Q.	Verbal I.Q.	Discrepancy
16 years ♂	100	96	4 points
14 years ♀	107	91	16 points
17 years ♀	113	110	3 points
and so on			

Whenever there was a discrepancy of more than 20 points in deaf children with more than 110 performance IQ I *always* found emotional maladjustment with an overloaded egocentrism, if not egoism.

What is the cause? Is that overloaded egocentrism the cause of the discrepancy, or the reverse? Is the discrepancy the cause of the egocentrism, or is there still another possibility? Is there a third cause common to both egocentrism and discrepancy?

I may suggest the following. These are intelligent children. They know more exactly what they want, what they see and observe. They do so keenly and remember it very well. Every child – hearing and deaf – now starts with a kind of egocentrism. But for a deaf child the danger of a prolonged period of egocentrism is very large, because of his sensory deprivation and of the fact that in the first years his language-acquisition is still very concentrated around his own experiences. We already saw, that the development of really personal friendship is retarded among deaf children. What will happen in intelligent deaf children if the language development is relatively too far retarded? First of all their language remains longer concentrated around their own experiences than normally, and with a lack of conversation with people of high cultural standard. Secondly, because of their higher intelligence their egocentric reactions, solutions and escapes will usually be more successful than in less intelligent children. So their egocentric reactions are more reinforced. The result will be a stronger egocentrism and also egoism. I think it can be expected that deaf children, who suffer from a big lag between their intelligence and cultural achievement, will show on the average higher degrees of egocentrism than others. This lag may hamper the development of authentic Christianity. I think that this is the explanation of the fact, found by Myklebust (1964), that prelingually deaf adult students of high intelligence, mainly conversing in signing, on the average showed a lack of 'insight', i.e. they were insufficiently aware of their own limitations.

V. AN ORAL MOTHER TONGUE IN REFERENCE TO RELIGIOUS EDUCATION

There are two forms of manualism – finger-spelling and signing. There is an essential difference. This may be illustrated by the objection of the schools' directors for the deaf in the USA against their colleague Dr. Westervelt, when he first introduced finger-spelling with the exclusion of signing in his Rochester-school in 1875: 'Ah well, Dr. Westervelt, so you think that you can teach deaf children English?' Indeed

40

signing is not English or Dutch or German or French, it is another kind of language, with another kind of syntax and with quite different semantics. It is known in the USA, as I have heard several times, (Riemann 1903, Stern 1907), that the students of the Rochester School reach an average higher standards of reading English, than those schools with combined systems. This experience has been confirmed by Quigley (1969), whose most important finding seems to be that those schools which went over to the Rochester method, achieved significantly better results in teaching their children to read than his control schools with combined methods. This seems to rule out at the same time the 'total communication' of McCay Vernon (1969).

I am not, however, an advocate of the Rochester method. I think that for most deaf children, including the multiply handicapped, the pure oral way of rhythmic speech monolinguistically used in lessons and free time, is the best method. This pre-supposes, that such a way of education is possible, the possibility being shown by real facts, which cannot be denied. If some schools do not succeed for one reason or another in this direction, they should not change the philosophy, but simply confess their lack of sufficient opportunities. My objections to the Rochester method are an underdevelopment of the rhythm of language, and an education directed too much toward a deaf ghetto (Van Uden, 1968).

So I will discuss now whether an education mainly by signs is an equal substitute for rhythmic, monolinguistic oral education.

That it is not an equal substitute may be shown by the findings of Quigley (1969) already mentioned, with regard to the Rochester method, which finding is congruent to a long experience in our Institute with regard to the pure oral way. This may be shown too by the results of such studies as of Stuckless and Birch (1964) and of Meadow (1968), that deaf children of deaf parents, who were not multiply handicapped and were above average intelligence, and who had an early communication of signing from birth, nevertheless were actually retarded in reading at 14 years of age.

The only thing I will now do is make you aware of some dangers originating from an excess of signing of our children and adults, mainly from a semantic point of view, with reference to religious education. The important point is, that a sign language is mainly a 'picture language' (Tervoort 1962), keeping concepts much too concrete and visual.

a. Schlesinger (1970) found that in a sign language there is a lack of *figurative meaning*. What this means for religious instruction may be

41

shown by this example. I wanted to explain to a deaf adult, who is intelligent enough, but too much dependent on signs, the meaning of the prophetic action of Jesus with the withered fig-tree (Mc. 11.21). She was wondering why Jesus could punish an innocent tree. I explained that the tree meant the incredulous Jews. 'Yes, bad Jews'. 'No, I do not know whether they are all bad, but some of them would not believe, were obstinate, and Jesus explained to his apostles how dangerous that was. Jesus pretended to look for figs. The figs stood for the fruit of faith . . .' All these things had to be explained one by one. I thought she had got it. Then I asked: 'Jesus was hungry. But for what was He really hungry?' 'For food!' 'Yes, He was hungry for food, but for what else?' 'For figs'. 'Yes, perhaps, but there were no figs. He was hungry for something else! . . . For another kind of fruit' . . . 'Apples?' 'No, fruit in its figurative meaning' (She knew that term well). 'The fruit of paradise?' She did not get it. I said: 'The fruit of faith' 'O yes, but there was no fruit!' 'Yes there was no fruit. Which fruit?' 'Figs' So she did not properly transfer. I could say to her: 'These meant the fruit of faith', but she continued to think in terms of the real tree and the real fruit. A few weeks later however I was able to explain the same parable to a deaf girl very easily, educated quite orally, yet not as intelligent (Performance IQ 100, Verbal IQ 94).

If the deaf think in signs with a lack of figurative meanings, expressions like: 'Jesus is the light of the world', 'Mary is the Mother of the Church', 'The house of my father has many mansions' and so on are hardly understood in their proper meaning. They remain to a large extent 'verbalisms'. So an intelligent deaf adult asked me, how it was possible, that the 'tree of paradise was at the same time good and bad'.

b. This dependence on images also appears in a *lack of generalisations*. This is always a danger for deaf children; it happens even in young hearing children. This may be illustrated by the following story of Piaget (1923): He asked a child of 5 years: 'Would it be possible to call this (a picture of a cat) a cow and this (a picture of a cow) a cat?'

Child: 'Yes of course!'
Piaget: 'Well this is a cat, and that a cow. Has the cow horns?'
Child: 'Yes!'
Piaget: 'But we called this (a cat) cow!'
Child: 'Oooo?' . . . (thinking)
Piaget: 'Has the cow horns?
Child: 'Yes, very small ones!'

42

To me that dependence on images in an iconic thinking is very much stimulated by thinking in signs. These signs become so identified with the concepts, that the deaf cannot detach them. This can be compared with the behaviour of the hearing child mentioned above.

Werner (1954) compares this behaviour of young hearing children with the thinking of primitives. Compare this with the following. The sentence: 'You have lost your friend's ball' was not understood. I investigated the reason. During the discussion with the child, I suddenly saw the 'thumbs down' sign. Thus the child understood 'lost' as losing a match! So the sign had misled the child. And not only that, it had fixed him to that meaning too, so that the child could not shift spontaneously to the other meaning, although it was very well known to him. He has been rivetted to that first meaning, expressed by a sign, which hampered all flexibility of thinking.

Let me give you a few examples to make you aware of the big danger which threatens the deaf.

If the sign for 'making' is something depicting the art of doing carpentry or building, what will the child think of such sentences as 'God made the earth', 'God made the dog' (cf. Bridget 1962) and so on?

If the sign for believing is something like thinking and grasping, take care that the children will not misunderstand, that believing is always something social ('We believe in God'), and that it has nothing to do with conceiving.

If the sign for son is a sign for male together with depicting the act of rocking a baby, take care that the children understand that Jesus not only was the son of God or the son of Mary at Christmas, but also on the cross and after the resurrection, etc.

If the sign for 'more' is that of adding, take care that ideas such as 'more love', 'more faith', 'more grace' etc. have nothing to do with additions.

If the sign for 'difficult' is something depicting a hard turning around of the fists, ensure that the difficulties of ideals have nothing to do with fighting or something like that.

If the sign for the Saviour is that of depicting the act of breaking the chains of bondage, make sure that the idea of redemption does not adhere too much to visual images of chains of the devil instead of including the real inner conversion. And so on.

c. Signing and the idea of happiness

Last but not least we would point out that 'picture-thinking' (thinking in images reinforced by sign language) is in its turn reinforcing egocentrism. So this way of thinking will hamper an outgrowth to authentic Christianity in too many deaf children. This may be explained as follows: How does the idea of 'happiness' develop?

The idea, the feeling of what happiness is (i.e. what kind of happiness one is aspiring to – consciously but in the main unconsciously –) does not have the same content in all degrees of development.

Each child starts with a kind of happiness which is very concrete, e.g. with a heaven where everybody is eating rice with golden spoons. The child imagines happiness in a rather sensual bodily way. In an egocentric way too. Even the happiness of living together with the parents is toned by sensualism and egocentrism to a large extent. And this egocentric imagery seems to be related to that concrete sensual imagery. Not that all this is bad! It is a phase in normal development. And as long as it concerns children, it will be accepted by others and even be good and natural. But not so after childhood. How does the child emerge from this egocentric imagery of happiness? This depends on his outgrowth, largely on the outgrowth of language, for he comes to the idea of ego by means of language. The words 'I' and 'You' and 'Mine' and 'Your' appear first precisely in his first 'negative period', i.e. his 2nd and 3rd years of age. At the same time, we see what part is played by conversation, because without conversation there is no conception of 'I' and 'You'. If there is a delay in conversation a delay in the outgrowth of ego can be expected. The escond step, that of 'ego-ideal' (das 'Ich-ideal') appears in the 3rd and 4th years of age, again mainly through language, in this case by the process of 'internalising' the rules and valuse of life. This implies that a higher idea of happiness is detaching itself from the foregoing mainly concrete-sensual background, within the mind of the child. But we have to wait until adolescence before that egocentrism is essentially broken through. At that time the child leaves himself, being ready to love another person more than himself, i.e. to experience that other person as a value and a centre of giving and receiving 'out there': the child starts to orient himself hetero-centricly. In this way a more advanced and enhanced idea of what happiness is originates, i.e. that we can be happy within another person. Now finally the idea of happiness has detached itself clearly from its egocentric background. Now we have the happiness of idealism, the happiness of personality. Alas not all human beings reach this higher idea of happiness, and many of them do so only in a crippled way, at least here on earth. This depends on many factors, for example on the environment in which the child is growing up. If that environment has a mainly egocentric atmosphere, it can be predicted

44

that many of those children will never emerge from their initial childish egocentrism.

'Picture-thinking', living outward, and the idea of happiness. When the idea of happiness (including desires, expectations, exertions etc.) remains too closely within the circle of concrete sensuality, then it does not detach itself enough from egocentrism. It can not, except with great difficulty, advance to unselfish love. The reason is, that it remains too much the captive of the more biological primary needs. This is the danger threatening our deaf children and adults, when they become moored too much to a mentality of 'picture-thinking'. 'Picture-thinking' makes them remain too long in a concrete sensual idea of happiness, and in that way, reinforces egocentrism. 'Picture-thinking' therefore hampers an advancement to unselfish love.

Let me illustrate this dangerous process by some examples from the field of religion:

The sentence: 'You will find rest for your souls' (Mt. 11.29) was for me impossible to explain to deaf children of 12-13 years of age of normal intelligence, at least not in the short hour of catechesis. The reason was a concrete 'picture-thinking' perhaps reinforced by signing. 'Find' was only finding lost toys (sign 'pick up'). 'Rest' was only lying in bed (sign of two arms crossed before the breast). The word 'soul' was unknown as 'not a modern word' (according to the teacher). If the same happens (and why not?) with ideas of heaven, virtue, love, hope and so on, what idea of being happy will these children have? How will they emerge from egocentrism? Remember, that the desire to be happy is the main basis of all our activities. An explanation on the 'means of grace' was responded by: 'How many graces? 10 or 20 or 100?' Once I asked a group of normal intelligent young deaf adults: 'What is a proper saint?' I got answers such as: 'He prays a lot' 'He flagellates himself' 'He preaches very much' 'He works very hard' 'He eats almost nothing' and so on. But the inner sentiments were not mentioned. Are they understood between the lines? I do not think so, at least not enough.

These examples may illustrate the danger, that far from an inner conversion of the heart being a goog basis of deep happiness, rather an external, too concretely sensual concept of happiness may be placed in the forefront of their feelings. Their thinking and imagery will be dependent mainly upon visual (i.e. external) respects. So we may say, that 'picture-thinking' will hamper the instilling of religion. Religion will be a one-sided service to them, something useful to them, instead of the reverse.

45

N.B. I must add, that unfortunately, many deaf children have to live in a more egocentric environment than hearing ones, i.e. an environment of deaf with deaf. This will also impede an emergence from their egocentrism. I call attention to the findings of Van Lieshout and IJsseldijk (1970) that those deaf children living in a family with other deaf children were significantly more aggressive than the other deaf, as already mentioned.

Sign language is in the main a 'picture-language'. Actually the oral language too has its onomatopoeias, but the difference is, that in oral language these 'mimicry-words' are exceptions. In sign language however they are the rule.

We must come to the conclusion that sign language hampers the deaf in their process of emergence from egocentrism to heterocentrism, and in this way impedes the outgrowth to authentic Christianity. To me the pure oral way, followed monolinguistically in school and free time is the best way of humanising and Christianising the vast majority of the deaf.

CONCLUSION

We spoke on the 'openness' of the deaf, which our Lord has put into the centre of their redemption. They should be open in real charity to God and men. They should also be open to each other.

Can they not be brought to a Christian understanding of their own deafness?

In the Middle Ages in France, the sick were considered as Christians with a specific vocation. So the Duke of Burgondy entered the hospital of Beaune, saying: 'Seigneurs malades, priez pour la paix' = 'Gentlemen, patients, pray for peace'. Very often I could explain to intelligent deaf adolescents, who had difficulty in accepting this suffering from God, that they had a special vocation in showing the value of a higher life to spoiled hearing people, that Jesus had transformed all human sufferings into sufferings of real self-surrendering love.

May the deaf be open to God, to all men, to themselves: 'Effatha'.

SUMMARY

'Authentic Christianity' is defined mainly as charity even toward one's enemies, an aim of education which cannot be achieved by indoctrination. 'Redemption' is seen as redemption from egocentricity. The difficulties of religious education concerning the deaf were explained especially in the light of results of research, which show their stronger and prolonged egocentricity. The basic thesis, that being accepted in love is a pre-condition to be able to give love, is applied to the principles of teaching a mother tongue. This last is taught by conversation, which implies first of all listening to the child, i.e. accepting him in his own personal value. How a child comes to love in the way he comes to his mother tongue is expounded. How conversation can be put into the heart of the whole education is explained. Religious education, including catechesis, requires conversational methods, otherwise religion remains outside the life of the child. Therefore a catechist is compelled to follow manual ways, if the school's standard is so low that an oral conversation is impossible. Nor can the catechist follow such programmed ways of teaching language, that a spontaneous conversation is hampered. For this same reason pictures cannot be the main means of teaching religion. Two respects of semantics are explained, the necessity of which is emphasised: the teaching of 'figurative meanings' and that of 'nuanced meanings'. It is explained, how this should be taught to deaf children. In connection with this the possibility and importance of reading (e.g. reading the Holy Scripture) is emphasised, especially for the intelligent ones.

The finding that deaf children and adults with a lag of more than 20 points between their verbal and performance capacities are endangered in their adjustment is interpreted. Finally the dangers of signing are explained with respect to figurative meanings, to abstraction and to the idea of happiness, proving the superiority of the pure oral way for the vast majority of deaf children with respect to their religious education.

LITERATURE

Anon, *Religiöse Erziehung für Hörgeschädigte Kinder*, Kettwig, 1968.
Berg J. H. v. d., *Wat is psychotherapie?*, Nijkerk, 1970.
Bloom F. (ed.), The psychiatric problems of deaf children and adolescents, *The National Deaf Children's Society*, London, 1963.
Breitinger M., *Die Erstbericht in der Gehörlosenschule*, N.B.T.Bi. 1968.
Bridget Sr. M., *Teaching religion to the deaf*, Mission Helpers to the Sacred Heart, Baltimore, 1962.
Büchli M. J. C., *De zorg voor de doofstomme*, Kampen, 1948.
Chauchard P., *La maîtrise de soi*, Brussel, 1963.
Frankl V., *Neue Folge des Vorlesungen zur Einführung in die Psychoanalyse,* Wien, 1933.

Fraiberg S. H., *The magic years*, New York, 1966.

Gentile A. and Di-Francesca S., *Academic achievements. Test performances of hearing impaired students*, Office of demographic studies, Gallaudet College, 1969.

Götzen H., in Anon, 1966.

Gregory J., A comparison of certain personality traits and interests in deaf and hearing children. *Child development*, 1938.

Hadfield J. A., *Introduction to psychotherapy*, London, 1967.

Harlow H. F. and Harlow M. K., Learning to love, *Amer. Scientist*, 54, 1966.

Hourihan J. P., Cognition, religious concepts and the deaf. *Proceedings. Int. Congr.*, Washington D.C., Gall. College, 1963.

Kagan J. and Moss H. A., *Birth to maturity. A study in psychological development*, London, 1962.

Kallman F. J., *The psychiatric problems of deaf adolescents and adults*, in Bloom (ed.), 1963.

Kates S. L. and Kates F. F., Social and non-social verbal concepts of deaf and hearing children, *J. abn. Psych.*, 1965.

Kay W., *Moral development*, Rev. ed., London, 1970.

Kohler C. N., Religious education of the deaf in state residential schools, *Volta Review*, 1966.

Lake F., *Clinical theology*, London, 1966.

Lewis E., *Children and their religion*, London, 1962.

Lewis M. M., *Language and personality in deaf children*, London, 1968.

Lieshout C. van, *Entwicklung von Beurteilungsskalen für das soziale Verhalten von Kindern*, 1970.

Löwe A. und Lauerer A., *Von Jesus und vom lieben Gott*. Ein frommes Lesebuch in einfacher Sprache, Freiburg, 1960.

Maesse H., *Die christliche Unterweisung in der Gehörlosenschule*, N.Bl., 1967.

McCay Vernon, *Multiply handicapped deaf children: medical, educational and psychological considerations*, CEC Washington D.C., 1969.

Meadow K. P., Early manual communication in relation to the deaf child's intellectual, social and communicative functioning, *Am. Ann. of the Deaf*, 1968.

Myklebust H. R., *The psychology of deafness*, New York, 1st 1960, 2d 1964.

Naffin P., *Das soziale Verhalten taubstummer Schulkinder*, Königsberg, 1933.

Nass M. L., Development of conscience: a comparison of the moral judgements of deaf and hearing children. *Child development*, 1964.

Ostow M. and Scharfstein B., *The need to believe. The psychology of religion*, New York, 1954.

Piaget J., *Le language et la pensée chez l'enfant*, Neuchatel, 1923.

Quigley S. P., *The influence of fingerspelling on the development of language, communication and education and educational achievements in deaf children*, Urbana, Un. of Illinois, 1969.

Rainer J. D., Altshuler K. Z., Kallman F. J. and Deming W. E., *Family and mental health problems in a deaf population*, New York, 1963, 2d 1969.

Riemann G. E., *Psychologische Studien an Taubstummblinden*, Berlin, 1905.

Sarlin M. B. and Altshuler K. Z., Group psychotherapy with deaf adolescents in a school setting, *Intern. J. of Psychotherapy*, 18 (3), 1968.

Schmalohr E., *Frühe Mutterentbehrung bei Mensch und Tier*, München, 1968.

Schulte K., Die Gebärde bei der religiösen Unterweisung der Gehörlosen in: *Mitteilungen Ghl. Seelsorge*, Freiburg, 1966.

48

Stern W. L., *Helen Keller. Die Entwicklung und Erziehung einer Taubstumm-blinden*, Berlin, 1905.

Stoevesand B., *Über Gebärdensprache und Taubstummen – Predigttexte*, 1957.

Stott D. H., *Studies of troublesome children*, London, 1966.

Stuckless E. R. and Birch J. W., The influence of early manual communication on the linguistic development of deaf children, *Am. Ann. of the deaf*, 1966.

Tervoort B. T., Esoteric symbolism in the communication behaviour of young deaf children, *Am. Ann of the Deaf*, 1961.

Tigges J. and Götzen H., *Kleiner Katechismus in einfacher Sprache*, 1952, 1959 Freiburg. Idem, *Biblischer Geschichte in einfacher Sprache*, 1959.

Tigges J., Sprache im Religionsunterricht, *N. Blätter für Tbst. Bi.*, 1963.

Uden A. van, Opvoeden van dove kinderen en missiegedachte, St. Michielsgestel, 1963.

Uden A. van, Das gegliederte Ziel der Hausspracherziehung, in: *Bericht über die Arbeitstagung Früherziehung hörgeschädigter Kinder*, Berlin, Aachen, 1963.

Uden A. van, *A world of language for deaf children*, St. Michielsgestel, 1968, 2d Rotterdam, 1970.

Uden A. van, *A world of language for deaf children. Part I. Basic principles. A maternal reflection method*, St. Michielsgestel, 1968, Rev. ed., Rotterdam, 1970.

Vergote A., *Godsdienstpsychologie*, Den Haag, 1967.

Weber K., in Anon., 1966.

Werner H., *Comparative psychology of mental development*, Rev. ed. New York: Intern. Un. Press, 1957.

Wilson J., *Education in religion and the emotions*, London, 1971.

Winnewisser A., in Anon, 1966.

Wrightstone J. W., Aronow M. S. and Moskowitz S., Developing reading test norms for deaf children, *Test service Bulletin*, Harcourt, Brace and World Inc., New York, 1962.

Zeegers G. H. L., *God in Nederland*, Amsterdam, 1967.

Schools and catholic education

4. Why catholic schools for the education of the deaf?

M. Nicholas Griffey

It is not necessary for me to emphasise that the Church in fulfilling the Divine command to proclaim the mystery of Salvation to all men has a vital role to play in the progress and spread of education. For education in the true sense of the word not only prepares man for life but enables him to live so as to co-operate with God in His plan for his eternal salvation. As Pope Pius XI put it: . . . 'Christian Education embraces the whole sum-total of a man's activity, sensible and spiritual, intellectual and moral, individual, domestic and social; not with a view to attenuating that activity but in order to ennoble it, guide it, and perfect it according to the example of Jesus Christ.' The aim of education then is the perfecting of man for the deepest possible encounter with God and as such it is an essential part of the redemptive mission of the Church.

In the 'Declaration on Christian Education' it is made abundantly clear that education in a Catholic school is the norm for Catholic children. It assures harmony and continuity with the Catholic home. In the Catholic school, parents, pupils and teachers share a basic attitude to life which affects all other attitudes so that home and school complement each other. As a result the child spends his waking hours in an atmosphere which enables him to get a right idea of religion. In school too the inculcation of Catholic religious beliefs and practices is achieved not only in the religion lesson but right through the curriculum. Religion is not looked upon as an extra to be tacked on to some already existing structure; its relevance and importance is often more easily seen in subjects like literature, history, biology and sociology. There is a Catholic way of teaching and learning, because Faith penetrates all aspects of life. Divine faith, as Father Cahill has said 'is at the very root of all Christian activity'. It would appear then, that there is a greater need for Catholic schools now than ever before, since in our secularist age false theories of education predominate. Besides in some areas there is a tendency to exclude all religious education from the schools, but neutral education is a fallacy. The documents of Vatican II mention the fact that the ideal situation is unattainable in many parts of the world where Catholic families have no Catholic school to call on for the education of their children. Nevertheless, the Magisterium must continue to show men the ideal and to direct them towards it. The point is stressed that the Religious education of pupils who from necessity must attend non-sectarian or 'integrated' schools should be the concern of the Church. Various approaches are used with varying degrees of success according to whether or not the pupil has the support of a good Catholic home. We shall hear more during this Conference about the provision of religious education for Catholic deaf children who for one reason or another are obliged to attend inter-denominational schools.

If education in a Catholic school is essential for hearing children then it is vital in the case of the deaf child. I am convinced that there is no substitute for the Catholic school for the deaf. By deaf children I mean those whose medical histories suggest either congenital or pre-verbal onset of deafness so that available sensory avenues for the intake of information are entirely different from those of normally or partially hearing children. Educationally these children present one of the greatest challenges to parents and teachers alike, because their disability imposes a profound type of environmental deprivation during the critical psycho-developmental period of childhood. A whole area of sense impressions is beyond their reach. Lacking the stimulation provided by the sound of the human voice in early childhood, the deaf child fails to learn language which is the highest form of human communication and the basis of man's mental life. The non-verbal world of the deaf child is one where thoughts and feelings cannot be freely exchanged. He may average or superior mental endowment yet because he lacks verbal symbols his ability to form concepts, to associate, to abstract, to reason, to imagine and to remember, will be seriously impaired. All these functions are essential if one is to come to a knowledge of God. It is true to say that the language handicap for the deaf child jeopardises his eventual apprehension of God. He may live in a Catholic home yet fail to come to know of the existence of God. During my experience with the deaf I have given religious instruction to a number of uneducated deaf adults, some of whom were highly intelligent. Never once have I come across one who of his own accord had come to a knowledge of the existence of God. There is a story of

54

an uneducated deaf lady who was admitted to the Catholic school for the deaf for religious instruction. First of all she had to be taught language. Eventually she received her First Holy Communion. On her First Communion Day she asked her teacher to write a letter for her to her brother who was a devout Catholic. 'What shall I say?' said the teacher. 'Tell him about God, about Heaven, and tell him that Jesus loves us all, because they know nothing about that at home'. Like the early Christians she wanted to spread the good news. What a relief it must be to minds imprisoned by deafness and lack of educational opportunity to come to the knowledge of God and His love! Another pupil who had had inadequate religious instruction reasoned in this way as she looked on a crucifix: bad people are punished, Christ was punished in an extra-ordinary way, therefore Christ was very bad! In the case of the hearing child one can without too much difficulty, convey the idea of vicarious suffering, but for the child who is utterly dependent on what he sees and feels this is a most complex idea. Yet an understanding of the Passion is fundamental for the believer. Not to know that the Incarnation is a temporal manifestation of a timeless Love causes spiritual starvation which balks description. Knowledge of God comes before Christian living and since the communication barrier caused by deafness deprives the child of the opportunity of knowing of the existence of God the religious education of the deaf may be looked upon as a special mission in the Church. Missionary work is generally considered as bringing the good news of the Gospel to those who are separated from us by distance, but who is at a greater distance from us than the deaf child?

In essence, education of deaf children is a struggle to develop language. What appears to be an effortless acquisition on the part of the hearing child becomes a frustrating and complex task for the child who is deaf. The normal child adopts our manner of speech; he uses words as we do; eventually he comes to think as we do. Language for him is not only a means of communication with other people, it is also a powerful means of communication with himself. Depending on the progress he is making he develops a sense of wonder, of enquiry, of reflection, of comparison, of ability to hold an opinion – in a word, he develops flexibility in using his mind. But language learning is exceedingly and distressingly complex for the deaf child, and educators of the deaf are still searching for the ideal method of teaching language. We are sure that language training must begin early and that it must engage the combined efforts of parents, teachers, supervisors and all those who come in contact with the deaf child. The approach must be consistent and systematic. Generally speaking today it is the teacher who teaches the mother tongue to the deaf child, though as a result of programmes in parent guidance, many parents are making a worthwhile contribution to this work. The ideal school for the deaf and the favourable home environment would afford the child abundant opportunities to use his newly acquired language skills.

Otherwise he will tend to use words as signals rather than symbols with resultant cognitive impoverishment. Effective teaching of basic language concepts is one of the most formidable tasks facing the religious educator. It calls for competence and for co-operation on the part of all those who are in touch with the child and a sharing of convictions and beliefs by all those in the home and in the school. Any teacher of language will insist on the essential vocabulary for the learner – words which express his primary needs and his daily experiences. The Catholic teacher of the deaf will make sure to insert words which will later on be gradually used to convey religious truths. Words such as: make, know, think, love, choose, pray, serve, obey, etc. will be part of the vocabulary of the children in the Catholic nursery and junior school for the deaf. Any Catholic teacher will necessarily consider himself obliged to teach such words. Many teachers experience frustration because they are not directly teaching religion in the Catholic nursery school, but every time they help a child to grasp one of these basic language concepts they are opening a channel for the flood of light and help that will come through grace and the sacraments later on. I remember a psychologist who carried out a survey on reading attainment levels in a number of schools for the deaf telling me that of the schools investigated only one which was a Catholic school, showed that the children understood words like 'adore', 'Worship' and 'obey'. He attributed this to the fact that these were words which they had learned in connection with their religion.

Presumably there was no religious instruction available in the other schools. For us language teaching and religious education can never be separated so that to a true educator in a Catholic school for the deaf one must be a competent teacher of language as well as a committed Christian. Language then becomes the key to the communication of religious experience, it helps to organise and clarify thoughts, it leads to the understanding of the moral code and the information of conscience. Like his hearing counterpart the deaf child has no knowledge of the moral code to guide him through life, because first principles are not themselves natural or innate, but like all intellectual knowledge

56

have their origin in sense experience. This is something he has to learn in his environment through communication and example with the aid of the grace of God and the Gifts of the Holy Spirit. While a deaf child is slow to learn language he is quick to become aware of conviction or lack of it in those around him. Their example and their ability to communicate with the deaf predispose the child to a certain way of thinking and acting. Transparent conviction on the part of teachers and supervisors in the school will lead the child to security in his inter-personal relationships which is a basic factor in religious formation. Eventually he comes to see that the words of religious teaching throw light on his experience of personal relationships and his response in personal attitudes. This is a slow, laborious and continuous task for the deaf child and his teachers. I am convinced that it can take place only in a Catholic school for the deaf because it involves a way of life rather than just a period each day or each week for religious instruction.

As I see the Catholic school it is a centre to which parents, teachers, and workers in the field of education, no matter what creed they profess, can turn for guidance, help and indeed inspiration. It is as it were a city on a hill, where the love of Christ is apparent to all who visit it. The Catholic school has many characteristics. In it our religion is lived in all its fullness, and the teaching and discipline of the Church concerning faith and morals are accepted. The teacher is the key figure in this school. It is not for me to emphasise the special vocation of the teacher of the deaf, because it will be treated fully by two eminent speakers during the Conference. The whole school is seen as a community of worshipping and serving Christians so that the children come to realise that love and worship of God culminate in Christian living. A liturgy adapted to suit the needs of the deaf child is the heart and centre of the school community. This will result in the inner vacancy of the deaf child being filled with trancendental reality. Lest anyone should think that this vision of the city on a hill is the vapourings of an excited religious imagination, let me say that it is not, for I have seen it realised in at least one school – in Sint Michielsgestel School for the Deaf in Holland. The ideal is achievable. It has been achieved, as I am sure those of you who have seen this school will agree. Where else in the world will you find a school for the deaf where five priests working on a full time basis cater for the religious needs of the pupils? Surely the Church in Holland is aware of its responsibility to the deaf.

The educational standard in the Catholic school for the deaf must of necessity be high since the language standard of the children must be such that they can comprehend the good news of Christ as given in the Gospel. Again because of the language handicap of the deaf the school is obliged to consider education as a life-long process. It begins at home, is developed in a very special way at school, continues throughout adult life and is achieved finally in the vision of God. The Catholic school for the deaf will concern itself with instruction and guidance suited to all levels – pre-school, school and after care. The school's responsibility to the deaf child begins with the parents in the pre-school days. They need help, and support to cope with a handicapped child. They also need guidance with regard to religious formation. In the school itself the programme of religious instruction is well planned to suit the psychological needs of a language handicapped child. The school is a place to which past pupils return for spiritual help and guidance. All this involves suitably trained personnel, hard work and continuous dedication. Ideally the school staff should include a priest who is specially trained to cope with the communication problem of the deaf. If the priest is not a full time member of the staff, then he should visit the school constantly and take classes in religious instruction. In this ideal school each child is treated as an individual. Particular emphasis needs to be placed on this because there is far too much stereotyping in our work. The aim is to enable each child to reach his highest level. The deaf child has to live in a hearing world; to do this he has to learn to communicate if he is to relate to other people. The level of his communication will be determined by his potential and his opportunities. For one deaf person it will be oral communication which will enable him to fit in better into a hearing world, and to help his fellow deaf who are not as gifted as he. For another it may mean manual communication and written expression. For many of our multiple handicapped deaf communication will probably consist of a crude signal system.

For all it will mean some form of communication. I have no desire to dwell on the oral-manual controversy but I would like to say that priests and teachers who work with the deaf should be able to use all types of communication. In this matter of communication for the deaf we should be 'all things to all men'. In the Catholic school all methods will be used in such a way that the child reaches his maximum potential. The children, their parents and their particular circumstances will be considered before any specific method is selected. The child with multiple handicaps will be our particular concern. As you know there

58

are more such children in our schools and in our pre-school programmes than ever before. Unfortunately we are forced at the moment to reject some of these children when they are presented for admission to school. I believe the Catholic schools should lead the way in co-operating with other disciplines in order to provide programmes for these severely handicapped children.

We need to be aware of this responsibility. In fact one of the most urgent tasks facing us is the definition of the reasonable limits regarding the types and degrees of multiple handicaps that can be served in the school for the deaf. Like Christ, the teacher in the Catholic school should be concerned about the handicapped and the underprivileged. Father Cahill has said that there is no specific reference to the handicapped in the Documents of Vatican II, nevertheless, in an address given by Pope Paul VI at the 1966 Conference of the World Federation of the Deaf which was held in Rome, he said: 'All that is of value in making the human personality more complete all that helps them to grasp the notion of their dignity as beings created in the image and likeness of God, all that can elevate them socially, culturally and spiritually: all this has the recognition and approval of the Catholic Church. It not only conforms to everything solemnly defined in the many documents and texts issuing from the recent Ecumenical Council, but decidedly follows the theme of the Gospel preached by Jesus Christ . . . The Church, because it is the extension and continuation of Jesus Christ, has the same mission as her Divine Founder'.

From time to time, we all wish, I am sure, that we could assess the benefits of education in a Catholic school for our deaf children. No doubt the effects of religious education may be among the imponderables but even so, it is tempting to try to judge it. In 1962 I was able to establish, by means of a questionnaire sent to 200 past pupils of St. Mary's School for the Deaf, Cabra, Dublin, that 98% of them attend Mass on Sundays. The age range in the group was between 20 and 70 – the majority being between 20 and 40 years. All of them considered religion important in their lives. A similar investigation carried out among the past pupils of Sint Michielsgestel School for the Deaf at about the same time showed that 95% of them were practising Catholics. The following are samples of replies given by some Irish respondents to the question: 'What does religion mean to you?'

'Religion means everything to me'.
'If I had no religion my life would be empty'.
'My religion tells me that God is always near me.

I like to think about this when I am alone'.
'My religion helps me to know and love God'.
'Without religion I might be led astray by bad companions'.
'I am grateful to my teachers because they taught me that religion is my greatest possession'.
'My religion gives me a true understanding of suffering. When I am worried about my deafness, I say with Jesus "Not my will but Thine be done" '.
'My religion is faith in God. It helps me to see beyond the present which is temporary'.

The deaf, despite their great communication handicap can be deeply religious if they are educated in this light. On the other hand in 1961 the International Catholic deaf Association carried out a survey on religion among the Catholic deaf in the United States. The results were depressing because they showed that only 22 % of the American Catholic deaf were practising the faith. Many reasons could be given for this, but the obvious one seems to be the inadequate number of Catholic Schools for the deaf in that country. Unfortunately most of the American deaf attend schools where there is no religious instruction available so that the children are dependent on what they get in their homes or in classes in religion provided outside the schools. In view of the language handicap of the deaf and the difficulties involved in helping them to become committed Christians it is no surprise to find that without full-time education in a Catholic school in the early years especially, they have no interest in religion. Likewise, English social workers for the deaf reported at a Catholic Conference held at Manchester, England in 1969 that many deaf boys and girls leave English schools without having had any religious instruction whatsoever. On leaving school they may drift into Clubs for the Deaf where the Chaplain who has had no training in the teaching of the deaf has to instruct them. One of the social workers attending the Conference very rightly asked the question: 'What does this minimal instruction mean to them in adult life?' From my experience with some of these adults I am convinced that they looked upon religion merely as a superstitious pratice – a ritual which is completely removed from their everyday lives. I must say that this was the attitude of even those who were highly intelligent. There seems little hope for improvement when we consider that there is but one Catholic School for the deaf in England. A similar situation exists in many countries throughout the world. One would like to know what is happening in the under-developed coun- the Chaplain who has had no training in the teaching of the deaf has to help? My ideal Catholic school will co-operate in such areas as: the training of teachers for schools in the under developed countries and the development in the pupils of an awareness of the needs of deaf children who are not as well catered for as they are in their own schools.

A study of the history of the education of the deaf shows that the needs of the deaf have to be voiced. They cannot speak for themselves. Since their handicap is so much hidden from the eye, it needs to be explained to the hearing world – even to Bishops, priests and religious in the hearing world. I would hope that as a result of the deliberations during this Conference we would become sufficiently determined and courageous to represent the great need for Catholic schools for the deaf throughout the world. 'Let us not fail in our duty to the deaf, so that we may receive mercy from Christ, the Father of the poor'. These are the words of Father Thomas McNamara, CM, the founder of the first Catholic school for the deaf in Ireland in 1846 on the eve of the great famine. In spite of all the conflicting claims on his charity in that disastrous time he still found it opportune to voice the needs of the Catholic deaf. Must we not also press their claim amind the crises of our troubled times?

QUESTIONS AND ANSWERS

Question
Does not knowledge of God and Christian living go hand in hand? Surely knowledge does not need to come before living.

Answer
Generally speaking it is true to say that knowledge of God and Christian living should go hand in hand. However, the total gift of self to God in response to His call (which is Christian living) is dependent on the assent of the mind to God's revelation of Himself. We cannot love God if we do not know Him. We cannot see God in our fellow-men if we do not know of His existence. Deaf people who do not receive education cannot of themselves come to a knowledge of God so that the pastoral responsibility of the Church is to present the good news of the Gospel to them in order to awaken their faith. When faith is activated then Christian living can begin.

Question
Why does the speaker use the term 'Catholic' rather than 'Christian' schools?

Answer

The title of my lecture was presented to me, so that I had no choice!! However, the terms are synonymous to me. It is interesting to note that the original title of 'Declaration on Christian Education' was 'De scholis Catholicis'. The necessity of the Catholic school as an essential element for a fully Catholic education emerges strongly from the document though reference is made to schools that might number Catholics among their pupils. (cf. 'Declaration on Christian Education Article 8).

Question

Make a distinction between a Catholic school, a Christian school, a Religious school and a non-Catholic school.

Answer

As already stated, to me the terms Catholic and Christian are synonymous. However, an inter-denominational school is sometimes referred to as a Christian school – that is if the teachers are Christians and if religious education is available. In some countries such schools are referred to as non-Catholic schools. A religious school is one which is run by a religious congregation.

Question

In some of our Catholic schools there are a number of non-Catholic children. What can be done for their religious education?

Answer

I think we have a special obligation to help the parents of these children to understand the language handicap of the deaf child so that they may be enabled to give religious instruction in the home. They should be put in touch with the Missioners to the deaf who are always prepared to help and to visit our schools if necessary. As teachers, I feel that we should be aware of what their faith demands of non-Catholic children in our schools. I am convinced however, that deaf children, especially in their early years are better placed in denominational schools. Emphasis on different beliefs will only add to the confusion which is the lot of every deaf child. Harmony and continuity with the child's home will be assured if the child attends a school where the entire community shares his particular faith.

Question

Is there a tendency to keep our deaf pupils on a lower intellectual level in religion as compared with, for example, the level we expect them to attain in literature? Could the speaker suggest a remedy for this situation?

Answer

In recent years this statement has been made frequently with regard to the normally hearing child. One of the reasons given is the lack of facilities for specialist training for Catechists. As a result catechatical institutes have been established in many parts of the world. While the statement is true in the case of the deaf child the remedy presents more serious problems. Because of his language handicap the deaf child is socially, emotionally and educationally retarded. For him, religious education is one of the most difficult subjects on the school curriculum.

I would suggest the following remedies:
1. The availability on a wider scale of guidance for parents from Catholic teachers of the Deaf.
2. Special training in the education of the deaf for Chaplains in Schools for the Deaf and in centres for the adult deaf.
3. Emphasis on religious education of the deaf in teacher-training courses, as well as careful selection of candidates.
4. The availability of short refresher courses in religious education for teachers of the deaf. It would also be a great help if some experienced teachers of the deaf could take a full time course in one of the Catechetical institutes.

Question

What are your views on the Chaplain of the School as a full time teacher on the staff of this school?

Answer

To me this would be an ideal situation provided the Chaplain is a trained teacher of the deaf and is suited to the work. One sometimes gets the impression that the only requirement for a priest who is to work with the deaf is facility in the use of sign language. This is far from the truth. Such priests need knowledge of, and experience in, the field of education of the deaf.

Question

Could you please develop further the ideas on children with multiple handicaps in Catholic Schools for the Deaf?

Answer

Since our aim in educating children with multiple handicaps is to bring them to their highest level I believe that we must discover their learning difficulties as soon as possible. Differential diagnosis and diagnostic teaching should then be available in the pre-school years so that a decision with regard to the most suitable method of communication to be used by the child can be made as soon as possible. Parents will then be helped to use this form of communication. Children with a mild mental handicap (IQ below approx. 70) and those with a severe language disorder may need to use a combined method of communication. The Catholic School for the Deaf will provide this. It will be seen to be concerned especially about the needs of Christ's little ones whose handicaps present such overwhelming barriers to development.

Question

Could you comment further on what the school can do to improve the parent/child relationship and identification process?

Answer

The first step is to help the parents to accept deafness in the child. For most of them the transition to the role of parents of deaf children is painful and unwanted. They need encouragement and support. They must also be helped to see the possibilities that lie ahead for their child. Generally speaking it is not fully realized how much help parents need in the pre-school years. Here the school can help by encouraging parents to visit the classes and to attend lectures given by professionals in the field. Once the child is admitted to school there is an obligation on the Head-teacher to see that parents get all the help they need with the development of communication in the deaf child. They must have it explained simply and clearly to them that the deaf child's idea of God's love for him will be based on his experience of love in the home. This will be a love tempered with subtle discipline.

Question

Does the speaker feel that the deaf tend to follow the advice of other deaf people rather than that of their teachers especially in the period after they leave school?

Answer

This depends entirely on the deaf person's level of communication. The young deaf school leaver who is integrated into his family and

64

who has friends among his hearing peers may follow their advice. At this stage he will tend to reject his teachers and all those associated with his school. As he gets older he may seek advice from his former teachers and from deaf friends especially if he has found it difficult to become integrated into a hearing community. On the other hand the deaf school leaver who has a low standard of oral communication will undoubtedly tend to take advice from the deaf community.

Question
At what age should full time education in a Catholic School for the Deaf begin?

Answer
This will depend on the availability of schools near the child's home. It is quite possible for a three year old deaf child to fit into a Nursery Class provided he can attend as a day pupil. In countries where children have to attend residential schools it would seem advisable that they should not be admitted before the age of four years. In such a case the child should be enabled to visit home as frequently as possible.

Question
You referred frequently to 'the ideal Catholic School'. Would you like to comment on the ideal Catholic residential school?

Answer
The ideal Catholic residential school will provide a home-like environment. The groupings will be small so that the children will receive adequate attention from adults. This is vital for the development of communication as well as for religious education. What the child is taught in the religious lesson is only of value if it is lived out in his everyday life. To do this he needs the example and encouragement of the adults responsible for his welfare. Man reaches maturity and consequently the full stature of the human person in community living, in bearing responsibility, in making free decisions and in being able to accept the consequences of these decisions. The development of these qualities in the deaf child can only take place in an environment where each child is treated as an individual by adults who are especially trained, and who themselves are committed Christians. In the Catholic residential school there will be happy teacher-child and out-of-school supervisor-child relationships. These personal relationships are the basis for religious education.

Question

The particulars you gave about the number of deaf adults who were practising the faith referred to 1962. In the last 10 years however, many changes have taken place. We are now not sure that all our Catholic teachers are in fact practising the faith. How will this affect deaf children? How can we help them to overcome modern dangers to the faith?

Answer

It it true that the weakening of faith among Catholics generally today is bound to affect the deaf. I had hoped to do a follow-up study on a population of Irish Catholic deaf boys and girls who had left school since 1962. It was not possible to do this but a pilot study did show that a higher percentage of the deaf were not attending Sunday Mass. In answer to the question 'What does the Mass mean to you?' one respondent wrote: 'An hour wasted on a Sunday'.

In addition to all the approaches to religious education of the deaf that have been mentioned so far I think we must now emphasise religious education for the adult deaf – especially for school leavers. In this area I would expect the well educated deaf adult to play a part in instructing and guiding those deaf adults who have not had these opportunities. In this way the deaf will be enabled to participate in the lay apostolate.

5. One approach to catechetical instruction of deaf children attending public schools

J. P. Hourihan

In the publishing business 'How to . . .' books are usually good items. Such books run the gamut of subjects from sauce to sex and the readers of these books, as do most people, want to succeed at something.

Educators of the deaf are no different. They, too, seek to succeed in their efforts to educate their charges. They, too, are attracted by the 'How to . . .' books of their profession – books which claim to have the answer to the perennial problems of teaching hearing-impaired children. Addressing himself to this phenomenon, a prominent educator of the deaf recently stated:

'No professional person has the right to believe or to state that he has the only remedy for a deaf child's problem in any area of his development and training. Too many times in the past, the field of the education of the deaf has been swept by "The Answer," which surges up into the headlines for a few years and then disappears into the past while new techniques, methods, equipment of organizations take its place.'[1]

For this reason I wish to preface my paper by stating that I have slightly changed the topic assigned to me from 'How To Give Catechetical Instruction To Catholic Deaf Children Who, Of Necessity, Must Attend State School' to 'One Approach to Catechetical Instruction of Deaf Children Attending Public Schools'. By avoiding a 'how to' lecture, I hope to impress upon you our conviction that different situations will require different approaches and what is effective in one situation may not be effective in another. Also by avoiding a 'how to' lecture, I avoid the presumption that the approach described is 'The Answer' to the problem of effective religious education in public schools.

In their efforts to maintain a parochial school system for the typical child the Bishops of the United States in recent years have faced a critical situation of rising costs and decreasing religious vocations, which forces pastors to employ lay teachers at salaries that in former

School expenses
As a percentage of income of a typical parish

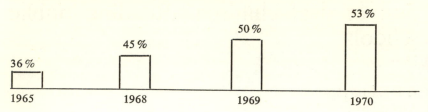

National enrollment
Millions of Students

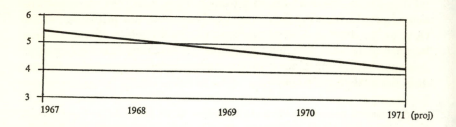

Number of Schools
In Thousands

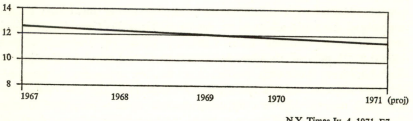

N.Y. Times Jy. 4, 1971, E7.

times would cover the cost of several religious teachers, or in some cases forced them to close their schools.

The situation has been made more critical by two landmark decisions of our Supreme Court on public aid to church-related schools, which decisions have cut off a possible source of revenue.[2] In the light of this

68

situation it is understandable that the development of programs of special education with their demands for specially trained teachers, for lower teacher-pupil ratio and with higher operational costs will be affected. Consequently, today there are more Catholic children in public or state schools than in Catholic schools. Those who concerned about the religious education of deaf children cannot look to the parochial system as the sole answer. The burden of establishing programs that will assist the parents of the hearing-impaired child must rest with the Confraternity of Christian Doctrine.

To understand any approach to the religious education of the deaf on the American scene, it is important to have at least a thumb-nail sketch of the general education of the deaf. Since its inception one hundred and fifty-four years ago educators of the hearing impaired in the United States have created a system of education that is unlike any other in the world. The Advisory Committee on the Education of the Deaf in its 1965 report to the Secretary of Health, Education and Welfare concluded that the 'educational system for the deaf is characterized by great variety'.[3] Mulholland had the same impression after surveying the organization and administration of day programs across the country.[4]

Deaf children receive their education in schools that are financed by public or private funds. Since this paper is concerned only about the former, the latter will not be discussed. Public funding occurs at three levels: local, state and national – following the political structures. In areas where special education is mandated, local school districts, which coincide with the geographical boundaries of towns and cities, have a day school for the deaf, or have special day classes in a normal school, or transport the children out of a district to a nearby program for deaf children. These schools and special programs are for the most part at the elementary level with the children entering at age five and leaving at sixteen. Local school districts also have deaf children integrated with hearing children. In such cases the school may supply supportive services to help the students achieve. State schools for the deaf are usually residential schools in which some students who live nearby attend as day students. These schools by reason of their history are educational enclaves which have children on campus from preschool to the high school level which could be an eighteen year span. At the national level the federal government supports post-secondary and college programs for the deaf, namely, Gallaudet College, National Technical Institute for the Deaf, Delgado Junior College and other programs.

The spiritual care and the religious education of the students in these various settings is dependent upon many variables – the interest of the local Bishop, the availability of a priest, the number of religious and laity who want to teach, the type of school, the method of instruction, the cooperation of the administration, transportation, financial support, parental support, etc. At Gallaudet College there is a priest who is one of the chaplains devoted to a full-time campus ministry. He is a member of a religious order which, seeing the importance of this work, has allowed him to work exclusively on campus. However, in order to support his spiritual programs for the students, this dynamic and zealous priest teaches several courses on campus. The state schools do not have full-time chaplains as does Gallaudet College. They usually have a priest in the diocese in which the school is located who, because of personal interest, gives part of his time to the ministration of the spiritual needs of the students. In many of these schools nuns, Catholic lay teachers and volunteers assist the priests in a program of religious education which takes place in the school itself after school hours. In many of these programs the method of communication will be sign language because most state schools allow its use. The religious educational programs for the deaf in these school districts function in the same way as do those in the state schools with two exceptions – first these schools as day schools are oral and second, the children may not be taught about religion in the local school because of laws forbidding such activities. This situation thus requires that the children be transported after school to some nearby facility, usually a Catholic school in order to receive religious instructions. Such an arrangement usually requires a motor corps, not only to transport the children to catechetical classes but also to their homes after classes. An alternative to this type of complicated operation is to have classes on Saturday at some centrally located facility to which the parents can transport their children.

In general it may be stated that most dioceses in the United States have some program for deaf students attending non-Catholic schools. These programs, typical of the education of the deaf, take various forms. Some may be directly under the jurisdiction of the Confraternity of Christian Doctrine; others may be under some charitable agency or organization such as Catholic Charities or the Mount Carmel Guild; still others may be the result of the initiative of individual priests or religious. Finally, some may be the work of apostolic laymen or laywomen who teach in a school for the deaf and, seeing a need, set up a catechetical program themselves.

70

The catechists who make these programs possible may be religious or trained teachers of the deaf but more likely are college students, high school students, seminarians, retired teachers of normal children, and interested lay people. The method of communication used in instructing the children is usually that employed by the school from which the child comes so that there will be no conflict with school authorities or the parents.

A program for the recruitment and training of catechists who will be capable of imparting the teachings of Christ to the children is essential. Recruitment of volunteers is not difficult because there are many generous and apostolic Catholics who are anxious to assist in such work. Personal contact is the key to successful recruitment. A survey of the area usually reveals societies, organizations and schools which would welcome an appeal for volunteers. Newman Centers on non-Catholic campuses, Catholic Colleges, Seminaries, and parish organizations have proven to be fertile soil for such recruits.

After the initial process of interesting people in the program comes the problem of screening out those who do not have the spiritual, emotional and intellectual qualities necessary to persevere in this type of work which makes so many demands upon the people in it. This screening is done through an initial orientation and later through a training program.

During the orientation, which takes place at the facility where the instructions are held, the volunteers are given an overview of the program, introduced to experienced catechists and given an opportunity to meet deaf children. For many this will be their first exposure to the problem of deafness. At the same time they are condidly informed of the difficulties to be encountered in teaching the deaf and are told that they must be trained for this job. Those who are willing to continue are then enrolled in the training program.

The training of volunteer catechists can take place at one of two levels – national or local. The International Catholic Deaf Association (ICDA) for the last decade has sponsored workshops throughout the United States during the summer months. These workshops have been under the able direction of Rev. David Walsh, CSSR, who has attracted outstanding professionals from the fields of religious education and education of the deaf to give the training required. At the local level workshops are arranged in some dioceses by the leader of the diocesan program. An example of such a workshop is the type that has been conducted in the Archdiocese of Newark. The workshop is directed by a trained teacher of the deaf. The areas of study are: the nature and needs of the deaf child, the psychology of deafness, special methods of teaching the deaf and religious visual aids for the deaf. As a text for such workshops 'Teaching Religion to the Deaf' has been found to be very effective for the level of volunteers that enroll.[5] The time spent in this approach to training volunteers has been proven to be well invested because it has returned high dividends by generating in the future catechists confidence in their ability to reach a deaf child, and by insuring that they know the proper techniques.

After the training program some may not qualify to be catechists. Such volunteers could still make a contribution as librarians for the visual aid files that each catechetical center has, or as teacher-aides, or as drivers in the motor corps which is always a necessary adjunct to any such program.

Training of catechists is important but it is not sufficient. For an effective program it is essential that the catechetical center have at least one professionally trained teacher of the deaf as a supervisor of the catechists. This ensures an instructional program that will adhere to the principles and the methods utilized in schools for the deaf. How can such a rare bird as a zealous Catholic who is trained teacher of the deaf be found? Again, by personal contact with personnel in the schools for the deaf. A visit to the administrator of special classes or programs for the deaf in the local school district or in the state school has always proven to be rewarding. Most public school educators – non-Catholic as well as Catholic – are anxious to have religious instruction and moral training for the children. They are only too happy to give the names of Catholics who are on the staff of the school and even arrange for a meeting with such faculty in order to have plans discussed.

Curriculae and texts are critical problems in the teaching of religion to children with hearing impairment. It was the experience of the Apostolate for the Deaf in the Archdiocese of Newark that the texts that had been written for the deaf were designed to be used by professionally trained teachers of the deaf and not by volunteers many of whom were not even teachers, let alone professionally trained. For this reason the staff set out to develop a text that could be put in the hands of volunteers – and, as it later developed, into the hands of parents. The end result was a book entitled 'Religious Instruction for Handicapped Children'.[6] Accompanying this book is a visual aid portfolio which contains pictures and flash cards to be used in each lesson. This text is the first in a series which is yet to be completed.

72

This text could be called a primer. It emphasizes with the utmost simplicity only the four basic truths – the existence of God, the Trinity, the Incarnation and Redemption. A glance at the table of contents will reveal that the order of presentation of these concepts is different from the traditional approach. The first lesson begins with Jesus and the concrete realities with which the child is familiar. (Some of the pictures depicting these realities will have to be changed in the Visual Aid Portfolio because of evolving liturgy, e.g. the drawings depicting the sanctuary). The book emphasizes the presentation of the basic concepts through units. Each unit has 10 basic parts: teacher preparation, materials, presentation, activity, story, review, enrichment, spiritual formation, homework and letter to the parents. The untrained volunteer is directed step by step in the presentation of pictures and flash cards from the portfolio.

This text and portfolio is a feeble attempt to meet a need. It is far from being 'The Answer'. It is fraught with problems. The problems are basically those of language. The questions raised by Van Uden concerning the 'constructive method' can be raised about the approach used here.[7] There is need for researching the present approaches. Hopefully, out of this international gathering will come a critique of present methods and materials that will give impetus to research in the future.

Even with the best methods and materials, teaching religion to deaf children can be an experience fraught with frustration when a catechist does not see progress at the rate found in hearing children. At such times he can be helped to overcome his discouragement by being reminded of how frustrating it must be to the child. The priests and religious who direct such programs will experience frustration too. But they must have a vision of the results. It might also help if they recall Christ's cure of the deaf man.[8] In the English text the translation states that Christ 'sighed' before his Divine action. In the Greek text the original word can also mean 'groan'. As one worker for the deaf stated: 'Among those who work with and for the deaf and who alone understand the difficulties in the apostolate, it is often said that our Lord groaned because He realized the problem. Exegetes may not agree but then they have never tried to teach the abstract concepts of religion to a deaf child'[9]

No matter what the difficulties, those in the work for the deaf – just as those in the work for the mentally retarded and the blind – are challenged because of their love for God and their love for their fellowman, especially those for whom Christ manifested a special interest –

the handicapped and the poor.[10] It is this Christ-like love that inspires us to go gailey through the darkness of the cavern of deafness ever seeking the light at the end of the tunnel. Perhaps it was this very love that inspired the Irish poet to write:

For love is like a plant that clings
Most closely unto rugged things,
And ever clasps with fondest stress
Deformity and barrenness.[11]

NOTES

1. Connor, L. E., The President's Opinions: Early Intervention. *Volta Review*, May 1971, Vol. 73, No. 5, P. 270.
2. In the case of Robinson v. DiCenso the Court struck down a Rhode Island law permitting teachers in Catholic Schools to receive up to 15 per cent of their salaries for handling 'secular subjects' and in the case of Lemon v. Kurtzman the Court struck down a Pennsylvania law which earmarked some revenues from cigarette taxes and horse-racing for textbooks, instructional materials and salaries in church-related schools.
3. Advisory Committee on Education of the Deaf, *Education of the Deaf: A Report to the Secretary of Health, Education and Welfare*. Washington D.C.: US Government Printing Office, 1965, P. 1.
4. Mulholland, A. M., *Guidelines for State Planning for the Hearing Impaired Child*. Paper presented at the Alexander Graham Bell Association Convention, San Francisco, California, 1968, P. 3.
5. Sister Bridget, *Teaching Religion to the Deaf*. Mission Helpers of the Sacred Heart, Baltimore, Md., 1962.
6. Reilly, Joanne and Hourihan, John, *Religious Instruction of Handicapped Children*, Mount Carmel Guild, Newark, N.J., 1963.
7. Van Uden, A., *A World of Language for the Deaf: Part I Basic Principles*. Rotterdam University Press, Rotterdam, The Netherlands, 1970, P. 18.
8. Mark 7: 31-37. (Knox translation)
9. Hourihan, John P., Working with the Deaf. *In All Things to All Men*. Joseph F. X. Cevetello (Editor), Joseph F. Wagner, Inc., New York, 1965, P. 89.
10. Luke 7: 22.
11. Drennan, John S., Love. In: *Love Poems of the Irish*. Sean Lucy (Editor), Mercier Press, Cork, 1967, P. 98.

QUESTIONS AND ANSWERS

Question
Instead of bringing children together for one short lesson or session per week, could not parents be brought together and trained to help the children?

Answer

You can bring parents together from time to time. It is very difficult, we have found, to bring parents together every week. When do you bring them together? You cannot bring them when the husband is working. You cannot bring them when the husband is at home because then he is with his family. Week-ends in the United States are usually very busy. We have a very serious problem in the United States of a high cost of living. In many families in America to maintain the high standard of living that they have, the husband works, the wife works, and the husband may even work an extra job on week-ends. So it is rather difficult to get parents together consistently week after week. We do bring the parents together once or twice a year – we have a Parents' Day and work with the Parents at that particular time. On other occasions our Priests visit the homes of the parents and try to work with them on an individual basis with individual problems they have with the child, and that is the only way we have been able to resolve it so far. Perhaps if we had enough money we could have closed circuit television beamed into the homes of parents of deaf children. That I would like to see. We keep trying. If I could get closed circuit television into the homes of all the parents of our deaf children then might feel we were making progress, but again I would have to have someone do a follow-up because television can never replace the teacher. You cannot get the spirit of Christ from a television set. I was watching the children and watching Father today, their little eyes were on him when he was going through the Liturgy because he is human, he is flesh and blood. He is with them and that is community. Television is a tool. It's good if we use it the right way, like anything else. If I give you a Mercedes Benz, or a Cadillac, and you begin to use that to transport steel beams and big rocks and boulders, your Cadillac and Mercedes Benz is going to collapse, for it was never meant for that use. It is the same way with television; it has to be used in a way that it will be effective as a tool.

Question

Could we have more details please about the short course to prepare Catechists?

Answer

We feel that this is absolutely essential, because it is not enough to have a zealous Catholic layman or laywoman working with our deaf children. You might be able to get zeal by osmosis you know, but you are not able to get the necessary knowledge to the children by osmosis, and so the techniques have to be understood. So we have to take them through our manual, show them how to use visual aids, and show them how to use what we call the Plymouth Chart. But, basically, we have to explain deafness to them. We have to explain that the problem is not speech, but language. We then try to get them understand that deaf children are not stupid, but that because of the deafness the learning process is slowed up. We then indicate to them why it takes two to four years longer to educate a deaf child than a normal hearing child. We also have to explain to them their own emotional reaction. And so this is all part of the training period, training them in our own techniques and how to utilize the material, above all to show them the materials that we have in our visual aid library, showing them how to use this equipment. You know, it's important to have visual aid equipment, but it's even more important to have the classroom teacher know how to use it. I remember, (when I was in a parish for nine years as a parish priest), a grand old housekeeper. She was a delightful lady, and the Pastor felt sorry for her – there were four priests there and at the end of the day she had to clean up a lot of dishes. So he went out and bought her a beautiful dishwasher. Do you think she would use it? She was afraid of it! And so we have teachers and we have volunteers who are afraid of visual aid equipment, because they don't know how to use it. We have to teach them how to use it, and this is all part of the training program. More than that I cannot say, other than to give you the course itself.

Question
Are all the catechists generally those who went to Catholic schools their whole educational life?

Answer
Most of them, not all.

Question
Do you accept those who went to public schools as well?

Answer

Yes, we take them from public schools also, but we try to make sure they know the faith. And even more than knowing it, we would like to know that they believe. I'm a great believer in nonverbal communication. The people that believe, as they are teaching, will show this belief in their eyes. For example, I love to watch Father Van Uden lecture; he is all involved – did you ever watch his eyes? The eyes, and the facial muscles and the whole body? He believes. You know, if I didn't agree with him, I'd love to argue with him, because I know where he stands. Well, this is what we want. We want people who believe, because when you believe, this belief takes over. The faith that you have takes over when you are trying to communicate that faith to someone else. That is when you are trying to be an instrument of God.

Question

How are the non-catholic adults attracted to the Social Center, and what is done by the Center in terms of catechesis for interesting them in the Church?

Answer

They are attracted to us because we obtain jobs for them. When the non-catholics are out of work they know that the priest has been getting jobs for the catholic deaf. The non-catholics come to us for jobs first. Secondly, the non-catholic deaf are as socially starved as our catholic deaf. They are in need of a social environment. They come to the Deaf Center because we have parties, dances, social activities for them, and they come there just to be with other deaf people. Now, on the occasion of coming, they sometimes express, on their own, an interest in becoming catholic. Today in the Seminary in order to prepare young priests for work with the deaf, we give two courses. We have a course in Pastoral Psychology of the Handicapped, and a sign language course. These courses are electives. The amazing thing is they are the most popular electives in the Seminary, which is very encouraging. We must be prepared in our work with deaf adults. By going out and visiting the non-catholic deaf when they are sick, by helping them to get jobs, by being as concerned about them as people of God, as much as we are about the Catholics, they then become interested in the religion that motivates the man to do this, or the woman to do this. And so, it is a question of bringing a Christ-like love to them. I do not go out with a Catechism in my hand. I never did that. I should be a

77

walking Catechism in that I should have embodied in me all that is in the Catechism, so that when I go in, all that Christ has given us, should be here within our hearts, and it should radiate in some way. They should feel it somehow, spiritually or some other way.

Oh, I might say something to you, Father Van Uden, for you mentioned an interest in group dynamics and interaction. We have taken the seminarians out of the Seminary for two days, and take them to Washington D.C., to Gallaudet College. We have them talk to the chaplains there, and to the deaf, conversing and communicating with them. That's the first thing. Then we take them over to the US Catholic Conference. The USCC is the most powerful organ of the Church in the United States. It is the headquarters for all the bishops in the US. So we bring all the seminarians over there. The bishop in charge of the Conference is a fellow-schoolmate of mine. And so, he, as secretary of the USCC, set up a meeting with all his assistants, the head of the Confraternity of Christian Doctrine, the head of schools and the head of every department within the USCC. Now here were these twenty young seminarians sitting down on one side of the table, and the head of the USCC, the Executive Secretary, and all his lieutenants on the other side. There was an exchange. What we were doing was getting interaction by group dynamics, and showing these future priests that one can work within the system and obtain results. And so, it is important that group dynamics be used so that they are not just talking to each other in the Seminary, but that they are getting out of the Seminary and talking to people about their interest in the deaf, while they are studying these courses in the Seminary. Would that answer the group-dynamic aspect of your question, Father Van Uden?

Answer
Yes.

Question
At what age is instruction for children commenced?

Answer
We accept them into the program around the age of six. They are in regular school at the age of five. We wait until they are acclimatised to the school environment and then we register them at six. Then it depends upon the child, sometimes it takes two years to prepare them for First Communion, sometimes it takes one year, sometimes three years. A lot depends upon the individual child.

78

Question
How are groups formed chronologically?

Answer
We talk about preparation for First Communion – that is one group. Preparation for Conformation is another group, and then we have a post-Confirmation groups which is for the teenagers. By that time they leave and go to the state school which is outside of our diocese.

The attitude of the teachers

6. What should we expect from our teachers: priests and lay-teachers?

A. Löwe

The theme of the paper I was asked to prepare was announced in the conference programme in three languages, namely in English, French and German. Everybody who is familiar with all three languages will have noticed that its precise wording differs fundamentally in each language. In English it reads 'What *should* we expect...', in French 'What *must* we expect...' and in German 'What *can* we expect... from our teachers?' Nobody in this audience will be able to answer the German version of this question. More or less, the same applies also to the French construction. I therefore decided to try to find an answer to the question in its English version, namely 'What should we expect from our teachers: priests and lay-teachers?'

We are all attending the 'International Catholic Conference on Religious Education of the Deaf'. The question raised, therefore, concerns teachers of the deaf and refers first of all to teaching deaf children religion. As we all know the religious education of deaf children differs very much. The situation in schools which are reserved for Catholic deaf children only is very different from the situation in schools where deaf children of all persuasions are being taught; or from the situation in schools where it is, for one reason or another, not possible to teach religion. Here, we are not only reminded of the situation in schools in the United States or France where religious instruction is not ordinarily a subject on the curriculum, but also of the situation in schools for the deaf in countries with a predominantly Catholic population like Poland or Hungary where state authorities do everything to weaken the influence of religion even outside the school.

We all listened to Dr. Van Uden's convincing paper about 'The Deep Influence of a Teacher of the Deaf upon the Character and View of Life of his pupils'. His remarks and also the arguments which Sister Mary Nicholas put forward to justify 'Catholic Schools for the Education of the Deaf' were in favour of Catholic Teachers of the deaf and teaching Catholics in Catholic Schools for the deaf. However convincing and conclusive their ideas may be – I am sure that everyone here will agree with them on most points – we must not nevertheless forget that the majority of Catholic deaf children are not educated in Catholic schools. This, for instance, is the situation in most schools for the deaf in the Federal Republic of Germany from where I come. At present, there are approximately 45 schools for the deaf in my country. Only six of them are Catholic and they are private. All six are comparatively small schools and admit also non-Catholic children. Only about 7 % of the total number of deaf children in the Federal Republic of Germany attend these private schools for the deaf.

For many years I taught in the state school for deaf children in Heidelberg. This school is open to every deaf child irrespective of the religious faith of his parents. During the time I taught in this school approximately 60 % of the pupils came from Catholic and about 40 % from Protestant families. The following remarks are based on the observations I made as a teacher of the deaf and at the same time lay-teacher for Catholic religious instruction at the school I have just mentioned. Most of you will agree with me that, on the one hand, it is much more difficult to teach religion in this kind of school than it is in a school were all teachers and all children have one and the same religious belief. On the other hand, however, nobody will doubt that it is even more difficult to teach deaf children religion in a place other than a school for the deaf, and this is even more true when religious instruction has to be provided by teachers who know little or nothing about the level of language and speech the individual child has reached or of the particular learning processes of deaf children. As you can see my observations were made in a situation which is far from being a marginal one.

After these introductory remarks I would first like to explain briefly what I mean by education of the deaf. In the past, education of the deaf referred only to the eight years of compulsory school-attendance. In Germany this concept is no longer regarded as sufficient. At present, education of the deaf begins with early training in the home, then comes the pre-school education period in a kindergarten and later special education in a school for the deaf. In principle, the period of vocational training and also of advanced education in adult age is part of the educational programme for the deaf. In other words: education of a deaf person starts in early childhood and continues more or less for all his life; it is a life long process.

84

What we can say about education of the deaf in general is also true of the religious education of the deaf in particular. Therefore, I will try to outline the situation of a teacher of the deaf who wants to teach religion and what else we should expect from hjm in addition to qualities that are required from the standpoint of compulsory education.

Furthermore, I would like to say some introductory words about the general prerequisites for religious instruction in our days. Whether we like it or not, we cannot deny that religion has lost its function of giving a comprehensive meaning to life and the world and has become a marginal phenomenon in the life of our society. This may perhaps be not so here in Ireland. Although 95 % of all children born in the Federal Republic of Germany in recent years were still baptized, only 20 to 30 % of the total Catholic population take a regular part in church activities. For this reason, we can no longer expect that the family contributes much to religious instruction in a large proportion of cases. The activities of the church reach only a small percentage of the younger generation who are the parents of the next generation of children. Also, religious conceptions which are mediated by the parental home, only in rare cases, coincide with what the Church means by them. The growing indifference on the part of society in religious matters is reflected in the fading interest which young people take in religious instruction when it is given in the traditional way. And the incongruity of the traditional image of the pious Christian with that of the successful man of our modern age as well as the pupil's continuous experience of the discrepancy between Christian postulates here and the 'Christian' reality there makes religious education even more problematic.

What I just tried to outline in a few sentences is not only true of the so-called normal family, it is also true of the family with a deaf member. And it is also true of many families from which teachers of the deaf are coming.

After these preliminary remarks I will try to find an answer to the question dealt with in this paper, namely 'What should we expect from teachers who instruct deaf children in religion?' By 'we' I think of all who are concerned with the welfare of the deaf child, all who take an interest in his religious education and all who speak on his behalf. We could therefore also formulate this question in the following way: 'What can the deaf child expect from the teacher who instructs him in religion?' *My first answer* to this question is:

Nobody among us would want a deaf child to be instructed by a teacher who is not prepared for this specific task. The child's parents would protest if they got to know that their deaf child was being instructed by a non-qualified teacher. From the linguistic point of view religion is the most difficult object among all other subjects into which a deaf child is to be introduced. From the religious point of view, it is *the* most important subject. Therefore, I do dare to say that good professional training is even more necessary for the teaching of religion than for any other subject. Thus, it makes no difference whether religion is taught by a priest or a lay-teacher. The deaf child has a right to expect that his teacher who instructs him in religion will be as equally well trained as any other member of the teaching staff who introduces him to other subjects. The teacher of religion should therefore follow more or less the same programme of study which is compulsory for any other teacher of the deaf and also take the same examinations. If these conditions are not fulfilled there is not only the danger that he will be fully acknowledged by the other teachers of the deaf as one of them, they will lessen the value of his teaching and perhaps also the subject he has to teach. The deaf child will be the first to become aware of this disrespect. I certainly need not explain what such experience can mean for the child's attitude towards religion.

Until now my remarks take it for granted that a trained teacher of the deaf is not only a qualified teacher but also a good teacher. This hypothesis does not prove right in all cases as we all know. Sometimes the deaf child has no respect for his teacher because of his general attitude in class. A visiting teacher, priest or nun may bring a heightened respect which then transfers to the subject.

Of course, I know that the fact that somebody has the qualifications of a teacher of the deaf does not necessarily mean that he is therefore also a good teacher of religion for deaf children. But the fact that he has received special training as a teacher of the deaf does certainly mean that he is much better prepared for giving lessons in religion than he would be without this special training.

As a qualified teacher of the deaf he should also know that early education of the deaf child is very important for the child's religious development. The sooner the child receives linguistic education, the earlier religious instruction can be started.

The main aim of teaching religion to deaf children is to convey to them the basic religious concept to create the fundamentals of their faith, to enable them to take part in Church activities, and to guide them towards a personal relationship with God. The burden of this task is heavy. And it becomes all the more so because the deaf child tends to revert to the real and perceptible world and has great difficulties in understanding the complexity of religious concepts and ideas. Until recently many teachers of the deaf tried to by-pass these difficulties by starting religious instruction at a late date thus avoiding these difficult concepts. Research done in the field of psychology of child development has however revealed the need for early religious education. This applies equally to the deaf child. Parents must be told that religious education is a *must* for the early at home training programme. Therefore, any teacher or priest who is instructing deaf children in religion must sponsor all efforts for an early educational treatment of deaf children. Should he still think that early education of deaf children is only a trifling matter (there are still teachers of the deaf who are of this opinion) he would deprive the deaf child, who is already deprived, of this so important early religious education.

Last but not least, I want to add that I know that many priests and teachers with no qualifications teach religion. Given a choice between a well qualified disinterested teacher and un unqualified but interested priest, nun, other religious or unqualified teacher I should prefer the latter. But I would also encourage the Church or school authorities to give the latter a fair chance to qualify properly for teaching religion to deaf children.

I also know of countries where the teacher trains 'in service'. I should not exclude such a person from teaching religion until he qualifies, especially if he is the only member of staff who is a Catholic.

Although I emphasize that the teacher of religious education needs to have qualifications, I may warn of the erroneous idea that qualifications are more important than personal standards or patterns of behaviour. *My second answer* is:

THE TEACHER SHOULD BE WELL INFORMED ABOUT THE LEVEL OF LANGUAGE AND SPEECH HIS PUPILS HAVE REACHED

The formal teaching if religion depends on language and speech. The deaf child must be able to comprehend spoken language via combined speech-reading and listening and must be able to use at least a limited spoken vocabulary. As a rule, the standard of language and speech necessary for the formal teaching of religion is seldom achieved before the deaf child has reached the age of eight. In other words: success or failure in teaching language and speech has its effects on the teaching of religion. The richer the vocabulary and the better the command of the grammar and syntax is; the greater also are the possibilities for religious instruction, which is predominantly verbal instruction. For this reason, we can also say that the beginning of religious instruction is also an important landmark as regards the standard reached in linguistic education. No other subject requires from the deaf child more language, abstract thinking and mediating than religious instruction.

This close relationship between linguistic progress on the one hand and religious instruction on the other hand has lead priests as well as teachers in a school for the deaf to conclude that the teacher who is best qualified to teach religion is the form-master. He knows better than anybody else what vocabulary each individual child uses. He knows which grammatical and syntactical forms the children in his class can already understand; he also knows how to develop new concepts and how to use them not only in religious classes but also in his general teaching programme. This is especially important in the child's first years at school during which formal religious instruction is not yet possible because the level of language development is still too low but during which religious aspects should already fill an essential part in the general language education programme.

The close relationship between language and religion can be particularly fruitful if the form-master is not only an outstanding teacher of the deaf but at the same time also a personality who regards teaching religion as a matter of special solicitude. If he is a Catholic he can prepare a variety of new concepts already during previous linguistic instruction, which he will need later in his religious instruction.

My remarks will have shown that I am convinced that at least during the deaf child's first years at school nobody else can be a better teacher of religion than his form-master. These first years are indeed very important years. They are not only decisive for the success or failure of oral education but also for the basic religious instruction and the role religion will later play in the deaf-child's life. We must therefore see too that during this period of informal religious instruction in which the foundations of language and speech are laid, these children are instructed by teachers who are in a special way prepared for this task.

My remarks will also have made it clear that I am in favour of oral education of deaf children. I know however that a purely oral approach is not feasible for a limited number of deaf children especially in several cases where deaf children have multiple handicaps. In the case of those deaf children, who for one reason or another, are not taught by the oral method, religion must be taught with the help of the same means of communication with which they are familiar. This means that the teacher of religion must know how to use such means of communication. I certainly need not explain further why the use of manual methods should be limited to classes in which there is a justified need for them. However, he must never use them in classes where deaf children are educated by the oral method. *My third answer* is:

THE TEACHER'S BEHAVIOUR SHOULD BE WORTH COPYING

'Verba docent – exempla trahunt'. This Latin proverb should never be forgotten in the education of deaf children. However important it may be that teachers of the deaf must be qualified for their special task and give sufficient consideration to linguistic aspects when teaching religion, we should not blind ourselves to the fact that the religious life of deaf children is not nourished and kindled through verbal instruction or delivery of knowledge only. Life kindles at life, religious life kindles at religious life. Therefore, a teacher who teaches deaf children religion must not only know what to teach and how to teach, but he must also be a personality whose behaviour emits rays that reach not only his pupils but also the other members of the teaching staff. I am thinking of such qualities as being hard-working, doing one's best, being honest in word and deed, being clean in mind and body, being polite, kind, sympathetic and understanding. If we want to develop these and other qualities in the deaf child, we ourselves must set the example. No teacher will ever succeed if he is acting on the motto 'Don't do as I do – do as I say'. His motto must be 'Do as I do'. Hard work, punctuality, tidiness, correct personal appearance, politeness etc. can only be expected from children if the teacher serves as a model. The opposite is of course also true. Children are the first to notice the good qualities in adults with whom they come into contact. They are also the first to recognize undesireable qualities. These are facts which we must keep in mind whenever we have to deal with deaf children. The best lesson will be given in vain if it is taught by a teacher whose personal appearance and behaviour are not accepted by the children. *My fourth answer* is:

Religious education pre-supposes baptism and membership of a certain church – in our case of the Catholic Church – and attention has to be paid to all the consequences which follow. The supreme teacher, the principal educator is Jesus Christ. 'Only one is your master – Christ' (Matth., 23,10). Christ has entrusted the Church with the task of disseminating his message. In the hierarchy the parents are the first to acquaint their children with the existence of God and the gospel. Many parents of deaf children cannot cope with this task. It demands too much from them, and after all we should not forget that very frequently their deaf child has to spend most of his time in a residential school. For this reason, religious education of a deaf child depends much more on his teacher and his priest than if we had to deal with non-disabled children. This again means that the influence of the teacher of religion on the religious development of a deaf child is probably much greater than normally. If his teacher has only a loose relationship to Church and if he is not actively participating in church life, this will certainly have its influence on the child.

In this context let me make an additional remark. The traditional task for the teacher of religion was perhaps seen too one-sidedly in the preaching or teaching of the revealed religion. One has, however, to remember that religious instruction is an engaged instruction which has to recognize the existent importance of religious creeds and questions. In so far as this relates to the personal creed of the instructor, this creed is then convincingly professed if it is blended with respect for other convictions and the pupil's freedom of decision which eventually is his and his alone. In other words: do we prefer superficial conformity or lip-service to deep convictions sincerely held?

The teacher of religion will have to present the Christian truth as a goal which he himself tries to achieve to the best of his abilities. If he wants to be a successful educator he will have to make every effort to maintain good relations with the children and adolescents as well as good contact and cooperation with parents and other teachers. Last but not least, he will have to use the best of the available media and exercise permanent self-control as regards his teaching programme. *My fifth answer* is:

If we want to meet the needs of religious education of the deaf we will have to realize first of all that this task is not limited to the period of compulsory education. Religious education is not merely part of the curriculum, as it is not merely a subject of instruction. Religion is not simply a classroom subject to be taught on a sessional basis but demands complete integration into the total experience of the child and hence to regard two or three lessons in religious facts or scriptural history as a teaching of religion is totally erroneous. As teachers of the deaf we have the obligation to provide everything needed by the deaf under our care. And the deaf entrusted to us want much, if not everything. They need us fully. Despite of all the difficulties they want to be thoroughly prepared for a Christian way of life. We must help them to find a way for their first encounter with God; we must show them how to pray; we must introduce them to Jesus Christ and the gospel; we must encourage and reassure them in their belief in God; we must help them to preserve their faith and strengthen it so that they do not yield to the temptations of life.

This task is not accomplished at the time the deaf child completes compulsory education. Therefore, a teacher of religion has also the obligation to keep an eye on the situation to which his former pupils are exposed after leaving school. By this I mean that the teacher of religion in a school for the deaf should feel responsible for and help organize and prepare services. He will, for instance, recite the prayers to the deaf congregation or deliver the sermon. This will however, become necessary when the officiating priest is not familiar with the special needs of deaf people.

The teacher of religion should also feel responsible for the organization and programme of social gatherings which usually take place after special services for the deaf. He should also help circulate letters to the deaf community. He should cooperate with the editors of periodicals or magazines for the deaf. Other occasions where he can give valuable assistance are home-visits to deaf families or elderly deaf people, which are organised by the Church. In Germany, some Catholic teachers of the deaf have written prayer books, and text books to be used for religious instruction etc. Last but not least, I want to stress that a teacher of religion should also feel responsible for adult-education which is gaining more and more importance. In other words: there is nothing which is not at the same time interesting from the religious viewpoint.

To conclude I want to point out again that we are living in a time of continuous change. The Church too is subject to changes. I do not know what Irish people are thinking of the new trends that are developing within the Church. In Germany, the majority of the Catholic population welcome them. Nevertheless, we should not forget that these changes came as a surprise for many Catholics. This is especially true of elderly people who need time to adapt themselves to the changes. The same is true of many deaf people. Therefore, we must act very cautiously and acquaint them gradually with the new interpretation of some aspects of our religion.

If we really want to fully equip the deaf child for the time following the school period, we cannot do without a good religious education, and the religious instruction should always be combined with moral instruction. The example set by Christ and his teaching, the sacraments he has given us, the miracle of creation, the interpretation of the commandments, the duties towards God and our neighbours should all be interwoven with a good conduct of life.

Far too often I get the impression that a lot of religious give catechetical instruction as a kind of insurance on the lines 'plant now, reap later' or 'be good, though miserable, in life so that you will be happy in death'. Religion is for living and can make for happiness in life but it is a divine gift to be cherished and nourished.

I realize I have left many things unsaid. Having spoken as a layteacher to an audience of mainly priests and brothers and sisters who are devoting most of the time of their life to God and to the religious education of the deaf, and thus also as a layman among experts I could therefore only touch upon some simple facts.

Finally, may I ask you to excuse my poor English which did not allow me to tackle the problems as thoroughly as I should have liked.

QUESTIONS AND ANSWERS

Question
'The teacher of religion must *never* use manual methods in classes where deaf children are educated by the oral method'.

There are some oral methods which follow a strict programmed constructive method. If one visits their classes one sees only a play of verbalisation of pictures and experiences, and/or a play of questions by the teacher and answers by the children. I am afraid, that if religious instruction to deaf children is given in this way, it will stay so much outside the life of the children, that the teacher will not reach his proper aim, because of a lack of spontaneous conversation. What do you say about that?

Answer
I know that a number of German teachers of the deaf follow such a strict programmed constructive method, which seems to me a too rational approach. The same will be true also of some oral methods used in other countries. I regret that I have to say that I see no way to change this in the near future.

7. The deep influence of the teacher upon the character and view of life of his pupils*

A. van Uden

INTRODUCTION

The basic idea of this paper is, that we, human beings, have no choice between belief and disbelief, but only of this or that belief or yet another belief. Our view of life, however rationalised it may be, is always dependent upon a lot of assumptions .

This happens in deaf children too. In the first section we will illustrate that deaf children too, come to some kind of belief spontaneously and also creatively.

In the second section we will deepen this in the way, that not all spontaneous belief is at the same time humanising. There are criteria for right and wrong beliefs.

In the third section we will discuss the belief of a hearing child and how it originates from a kind of symbiosis with his parents.

In the fourth and last section we will discuss the deep influence of a teacher of the deaf, which can be compared in many respects with that of the parents.

I. DEAF CHILDREN OBTAIN A KIND OF BELIEF SPONTANEOUSLY

Deaf children are normal human beings. There seems to be no essential difference between deaf and hearing children in respect of their reactions to the universe and to the secrets and mysteries of our human existence. The only point is, that these reactions can remain too primitive for a longer period of life, and so they can be moored deeper in the unconscious life than with hearing children, which can produce strange fears even in adult life. For instance deaf children believe in Santa Clause much longer than hearing children; a deaf adult told me

* For literature see pag. 47.

94

that he was somewhat afraid of his mother after her death; deaf adults may use medals, holy water, images and so on more as fetishes than as a symbolic and graceful help for conversion.

Some anecdotes may illustrate how deaf children sometimes think in their beliefs:

An intelligent deaf child of 8 years of age thought – as she told me later – that every night God came from heaven and pulled all the blades of grass up a little bit, so that they showed a bit longer next morning. It took about 3 years for her to get rid of this idea.

Another deaf child of about 9 years of age thought, that there were small gaps in the blue heaven, through which the light of heaven beamed; these gaps were the stars.

One afternoon in summertime, Dr. Maesse tells us, (1967), it was very dark: a thunderstorm threatened. Rather suddenly the storm broke. The children (2nd grade) were very afraid and silent. A girl said: 'Larm! man up!' She did not ask this. She had persuaded herself that this was so.

A child was blaming another child (both about 10 years of age) for saying that he would eat a lot of chocolates in heaven: 'There will be plenty of all kinds of candies' .On a hot day they asked the teacher whether it would be warm or cold in heaven.

Some boys of 12 years of age had a hot discussion on lightning. One party said: it was two clouds bumping each other. The other party said: 'No, it is two stars bumping into each other'. The wise brother was asked to solve the problem. They asked him: '*Who* does that? God? An Angel?'

Other children of about the same age thought that the wind came from the moving trees. But the big problem was, *who* was really moving all these big trees! (We draw attention to that question-word: 'Who)'.

All this is of course rather childlike. More serious however is an image of God as if He were our servant instead of the inverse, i.e. a rather egocentric image of God, which rules out more or less the most important feeling of real love. This image of God becomes then a primitive mixture of fear and egocentrism. For instance some deaf adults came back from a pilgrimage to Lourdes, rather angry, that not one miracle had taken place . . . 'And we have paid so much for that!' I found this attitude, especially in male people, rather often connected with stinginess and a very rigid way of life, maintaining rules very strictly, and when married, with an overbearing dominant attitude towards their wives.

The Holy Scripture handles two definitions of faith:

a. Hebr. 11.1 'The faith is the basis of what we hope, the argument of the reality of the invisible things'. (It is that which gives substance to our hopes which convinces us of things we cannot see)

b. A more personal faith as a personal surrender, e.g. Rom. 10.14: 'How can we invoke Him (God) without first believing *in* Him?' In the same sense: 'Your faith has saved you' (passim in the Gospels).

The first definition is more general and can be applied to many kinds of belief. For instance atheists too are convinced of a future of happiness for all men of body and mind, i.e. they base themselves on a grounding of fanatic hope for things which are invisible.

Every human being lives on a foundation of belief: strict disbelief is impossible. Everybody starts with some suppositions, often quite unconsciously, which he assumes without a possibility of proving them in a strict sense. Also when somebody says, 'I believe only what I see and nothing else', he confesses a special belief, that there *is* nothing else worthwhile believing in or worthwhile looking for. This assumption cannot be proven. And in a psychological sense Ostow and Scharfstein (1953) emphasised that there is a 'need to believe'. We look for a basis to our hopes and wants and wishes. We also look for consonance in our behaviour and in the ideas we have about the universe. We look for a meaning for all things and we assume meanings unless we reject them purposely. We always in some way rationalise our world.

Our conclusion is, that a quite neutral education is absolutely impossible. If we educate a child, either hearing or deaf, without teaching it any belief (which in itself is already contradictory: if we meet a child we teach it, even without saying any word), it will almost automatically develop its own belief. It will develop its own philosophy of life, its own way of life, right or wrong.

Mainly we can say incorrectly, because a human being will be misled so often by his own congenital egocentricity: 'I don't do the good I want to do; my own actions bewilder me, what I do is not what I wish to do'. (St. Paul Rom. 715).

So we don't make a child really happy if we don't teach it faith or belief. The child looks for that and seeks help. He has a 'need to believe', and here we can add, that the faith in God the Father of all men, and the faith in a universal love also of our enemies, is the only faith which does not include indoctrination, i.e. does not include a narrowness of mind. So there is no danger at all in teaching children *this* belief. On the contrary this belief is the only truly redeeming one, quite suited to our human nature.

So Jung (quot. Lewis 1962, pag. 14) is right in saying: 'Even the most primitive of peoples have never been as natural as the animals are'. There is always some culture, and we may add again, that men, left to themselves, don't find their really humanising faith. In an interesting experiment (cf. Fraiberg 1963), psychologists have tried to educate children from birth without any impression of fear or dread. In spite of this these children developed fears in their own minds. This prevention appeared to be quite impossible, in the same way in which it is impossible to educate a child without the impression of any specific love and/or hatred. If we don't educate it to a universal love (= charity) it will almost automatically develop another love, that of egoism, i.e. it will not be redeemed from the tyranny of the 'flesh' (NT passim). To make a comparison: It is impossible to keep a cup empty: if it is emptied of wine, it is immediately filled with air. Our co-operation with the redemption of Christ is therefore to prevent our deaf children acquiring a wrong belief, inspired by egocentricity and narrowness of mind. How can this be done? First of all by giving these children our own open-minded charity.

There is a very deep psychological law, already found in primates (Harlow 1966), that accepting love is bringing to love, and that not being accepted in love brings an organism to hatred. This looks a strange thing: being loved, i.e. loved by truly open-minded love, could be expected to lead to egocentricity. The inverse is true.

Perhaps this is the reason why so many psychiatrists and psycho-therapeutists maintain, that a trusting faith in God our Father in heaven is an important predisposition to prevent and cure neuroses (Frankl 1933, Lewis 1962, Lake 1966, Vergote 1967, Chauchard 1967, Hadfield 1967, Van den Berg 1970). The feeling of ultimately being accepted by Reality, i.e. by God the source of all reality, is the main basis of a healthy life and the cure of all fears.

III. BELIEVING OF A CHILD ORIGINATES FROM A 'SYMBIOSIS' WITH THE PARENTS

The 'need to believe' seems to be strongly connected with the 'affiliation-need'.

What 'affiliation-need' is, may well be illustrated by the behaviour of a faithful dog, which feels it has done something that displeases his master. It caresses its body against the legs of his master and remains faithful even when beaten. In the same way a child starts with an enormous love and surrender to his parents: this is biologically based. And a disappointment in this field always means a psychic, and very often a psychosomatic trauma. The rearing period of the child usually determines a whole life of a human being in many fundamental respects. This implies a world of meanings given to persons and things, consciously and perhaps more unconsciously and without reflection. This world of meanings, wherein we live, grow and die, has been built up from early childhood, starting from the periods of which we are not all aware by an overwhelning sea of classic and operant conditions. We govern over life through that sea, which never stops working but always grows further and charges too. To give an illustrative example: you have lived in a village with a small church for the first five years of your life. The small church is the one you visited with your father and mother. At five years of age you left that village. The whole family moved to a town 100 kms. away. You did not visit the village again. You got married and had children. Your parents died. After 50 years you pay a visit to the village. Your birthplace and its small garden are still there. Its church is still there too. When you enter that house and that church you are overwhelmed with feeling: a whole concatenation of reflexes and responses comes over you. These places, although seemingly forgotten, did not lose their mainly unconscious meanings, so strong that you are almost overpowered. These reactions are not only spiritual, they are mainly bodily, psychosomatic: your whole body and mind is involved.

So the bearing is quite naturally continued in the rearing with deep affiliation and symbiosis of parents and child. We should not say: 'The parents have a *right* to educate their children according to their own conviction'. It is more of a biological impossibility for them to do otherwise.

Language and conversation play an important part in all this of course, but not only language, not even just conscious expressive movements, it is more of a whole symbiosis. I know some parents follow the philosophy of leaving their children free especially in religious affairs. They themselves live more or less according to a religious conviction, but do not recommend it, at least not consciously, to their children. They think they give their children a full freedom of choice. Whether they succeed in such a treatment seems to be very doubtful.

It can have three effects. Either the child imitates his parents, but without deep conviction because it is not helped that way, or it looks for exactly the opposite, or it does not understand the parents' meaning of leaving him a free choice and will lose part of his confidence.

These effects seem to be suggested by a Dutch interconfessional sociologic investigation (Zeegers 1967) using a questionnaire. One of the questions was: 'Do you have a need to pray?'

Respondents	%	yes		
Members of a Confession	91	%	±	2.2
Not Members of a Confession but educated in a Confession	39	%	±	5.1
Not Members of a Confession and not educated in a Confession	18.5	%	±	4.2

The figures for 'yes' to the questions 'Do you prefer a confession for your children?' 'Do you believe in Divine Providence?' and the like, were similar. Only 8.5 % of those, not educated in a confession, came to a confession later in life; those educated in a confession, maintained that or another confession for 69 %. These differences were all significant $p < 0,01$ (less than 1 %).

There is, however, also a difference between bearing and rearing. In bearing it is mainly the mother who actively influences the child. In rearing there is a growing *co*-partnership. Not only the mother influences the child, but the reverse is true too: as soon as the mother and father see their new born baby, this baby influences them: the baby grows to a new ego, facing them. The child has his own contribution to make: there is a real *sym*-biosis. Consequently the influence of parents becomes more and more educational, i.e. dialogic, not so much imprinting but more evoking, preparing the conditions for free reactions. This symbiosis includes a specific image of the world of the child: it develops specific meanings to persons and things. So a deaf girl of 6 years of age was afraid of all males because the father did not accept her: this behaviour could be corrected by modifying the behaviour of the father. A deaf boy was remarkably disinterested in cars, unlike other children, perhaps because his parents had a taxi-service.

We said that parents become more and more aware of their child as a new ego. If not, there may grow a very dangerous attitude of egocentricity in both parents and child. But on the other side the child becomes more and more aware of the ego of the parents, not only because they sometimes frustrate his desires and wants by commands and prohibitions, but also because he detects, that his father and mother have definite interests outside him. Every child starts unconsciously with the idea and feeling, that his father and mother exist only for him. This idea later becomes more and more resolved. He detects that his parents have friends and leave him at home, perhaps in the care of someone else, in order to visit their friends. He detects that his father and mother are in love with each other. These are very important detections, and for some children, especially for children with some degree of affective neglect, they may be almost unbearable. It can happen that a child rejects the friends of his parents, that he hates one of the parents or both, and so on. All this implies again a change in his world of meanings. This human symbiosis therefore appears to affect not only child and parents, but the whole social setting, including the church, and the world of ideals and fears. Let us apply these principles now to religious education. We would summarise them in two ways:

Indirect Influence: How is the image of God influenced by parent-child relationships?

Direct Influence: How do parents influence that image of God more directly?

a. How is the image of God influenced by parent-child relationships?

We would express this influence as follows: God is a most vulnerable projection-screen of the parent-child relationships. As we have already mentioned: a child can reject or accept for instance his parents' friends because of a wrong or a right parent-child relationship. This friend is in some way the projection-screen of the child's bad or good feelings to his parents. In the same way God is a projection-screen for these feelings, assuming of course that the idea of God plays a part in the life of the family. But God is a more vulnerable projection-screen. Let us assume, that the bad relationship between certain parents and their child results in a rejection or maltreatment of an uncle by that child. This rejection can be corrected: for instance the uncle can gladden the child by giving him presents, by embracing him, etc. The child *experiences* then that that uncle is not as bad as his image told him. It can happen that some good educators give a child a better 'experience of God' than he had imagined. But you feel that here 'experience of God' is much more indirect than that of the uncle. So we must say that God is a very vulnerable projection-screen for the parent-child

100

relationships. The same must be said of the image of Christ, for instance of the Sacred Heart, the image of our Lady, and so on. As an example, a child who suffered from a serious affective neglect went to Lourdes with his parents, and said that 'the statue of our Lady in the grotto had a sneering expression' (Lewis 1962).

Consequently I fully agree with the words of the English psychologist Lewis (1962): 'If the child's infantile images of God, of Christ, of the Virgin have been based upon an experience of parents who are strong, loving, just, merciful and spiritually mature, everything that comes later in his religious life will be an enrichment and confirmation of his faith. But if, on the other hand, his early experiences have been of parents who have been weak, indifferent, untrustworthy, over-indulgent or even illtempered, the later images which he forms of the divine Persons must remain shallow, unstable and open to doubt. It may well be that the negative images will disappear from consciousness; but they will inevitably persist in the unconscious, charged with negative feelings. Then, as the child's religious life deepens, they are a constant danger to it. It cannot be otherwise . . .' In my work (Lewis) I have encountered a number of adolescents who were in difficulties over their religious life. Always their story was basically the same . . . In every case we found that an important factor in the situation was a faulty relationship with one or other of the parents. They unconsciously expected God to behave as their parents. If the young people had become soft through overindulgence and overprotection during infancy and middle childhood, they expected a God granting all their wishes and shielding them against every possible hardship. At the other extreme were the children of indifferent, harsh or dominating parents. As soon as things began to go wrong for them, the image of an angry God who punished mercilessly, and who even delighted in disappointing and frustrating, erupted from the unconscious'.

b. How do parents influence an image of God more directly?

It seems to be unthinkable that this influence will contradict the unconscious influence, described above. Consequently it will be more or less a confirmation of the impressions the child has developed for himself from the parent-child relationship. This direct influence will be mediated mainly by language, for instance by the way one talks of God, of the Saints, of the church, guided by the newspapers, television etc. or not. This includes the way of reacting to happenings. For instance a father suffering from a heart disease said: 'It will serve some useful purpose'. A mother said after an accident involving a member of the family: 'He deserved it' . . .

Very important, however, is the way in which the parents teach their children to pray, including the example they give. We speak here of praying only in the sense of real 'talking with God' and not of a thoughtless pattering of a series of Hail Mary's, of automatically making the sign of the cross and so on. The existence of God as a reality with meaning for himself personally is mostly detected by the child during the individual prayers of his father and mother (Vergote 1967). Instance the following behaviour of a small (hearing) child in the church. He was old enough to accompany his parents to Mass, but not to receive Holy Communion. The father and mother went to Communion. The child looked and looked. They came back and closed their eyes to pray. The child detected that his mother was involved in something better or 'Somebody', God, Christ, outside him. He gently nudged his mother to draw attention to himself. Mother told him to be quiet: She had to talk with Jesus. 'No' said the boy, 'Jesus is mine'. It seems to be clear that the parent-child relationship is projected to Christ, as a screen. This influences the concept of prayer. If the parent-child relationship is right, these experiences will be well integrated and enrich the child in his own praying. If not, the effects may be disastrous.

Very important too are the moments when the parents stimulate a child to pray. I call attention to the intentions for which the child is requested to pray. Are these only wordly and egocentric? Are they somewhat magic, i.e. somewhat extorting without humbleness? Is thanksgiving always forgotten? The times the child is requested to pray: is it only incidentally or only customary, only in periods of danger? Listen to this utterance of a mother: 'Now you must pray, because you cannot do it yourself!' Such an exhortion just develops an image of a 'God filling the gap'. Listen to two children before the door of the chapel the morning of their examination. First child: 'I will pray a little bit'. Second child: 'I don't need it. I know enough'.

Our conclusion is: our task as educators of the deaf is not finished with school and boarding school. We should integrate our work with that of the parents. We educate the children for the parents, do we not?

IV.   THE DEEP INFLUENCE OF A TEACHER OF THE DEAF

Our influence on our deaf children can be compared with that of the parents to a great extent. Many instances, mentioned above, could be repeated here.

Every Catholic school, whether it be for hearing or deaf children, is an extension of the parents and of the Church, or better of the parents within the Church, of their Holy Marriage. But this is true of schools for the deaf in a very specific way. Perhaps a teacher of normally hearing children may dismiss his personal religious and/or philosophic attitudes. Perhaps a teacher of normal hearing children can pose as a pure instructor, denying that he is an educator. This seems to be impossible for a teacher of the deaf, at least not in our conversational way of teaching. The reason is that we have to teach deaf children their mother-tongue. We meet here the same influence on the children as mentioned with the parents: an indirect unconscious influence, indeed a kind of symbiosis; a direct influence.

But first we have to answer this question: Has a teacher of the deaf actually some *duties* in the religious instruction of deaf children?

There are chaplains as well as teachers who say 'No'. Both groups say: 'This is only the responsibility of the delegated catechist'. I think that firstly the delegated catechist should be a fully-qualified teacher of the deaf himself. Secondly, the teacher of the classroom, unless he himself is a qualified catechist, should co-operate with the catechist.

We saw in the first paper, that catechesis from the lowest to the highest grades presupposes a lot of language-acquisition. The teacher in the classroom as well as the house-parents have to know what the modern requirements of religious education and instruction are. This is the job of the expert catechist. If he is a priest the liturgic education can be involved. If not, there should be a co-operation between priest, catechist, teacher of the class and house-parents.

Consequently I think that a separation of catechists from the school, i.e. from the language-acquisition, is not an acceptable design. Kohler (1966) found, that 40.6% of the State Residential schools in the USA had no programme at all for catechesis in co-operation with the school. Some of them gave only a few opportunities to a chaplain or pastor or someone else, who were not teachers of the deaf, to teach religion outside the school hours. If also, these same children have little linguistic connection with their parents (as has been found by Stuckless and Birch, 1964, in too many hearing parents of deaf children in these schools) it must be said that these children are left to themselves; they grow up without any religious instruction, i.e. without any revealed faith. They will develop their own beliefs, whether or not instigated by their deaf friends.

I do not agree with the philosophy that should the teacher give good language, the catechist can suffuse it with religion. No, the language should be prepared in the direction of the catechesis and the catechesis should be elaborated in the language-lessons. We already saw that this is not detrimental to language-acquisition, in fact precisely the inverse. So, I see the catechesis as the jewel in the setting of the whole education: Education of the deaf is similar to mission work in the under-developed countries.

Is there an *indirect*, mainly unconscious, influence of the teacher of the deaf on his children?

Yes there is, especially when a real conversational approach is followed.

We will emphasise the powerful weapon in the hands of a teacher of the deaf to prevent or correct bad influences of some parents who fail in their educational task.

His 'seizing' method of accepting the child fully, appeared to be a very important therapy for such children (in our Institute about 20 % in different degrees) suffering from the 'desolation syndrome' or 'affective neglect'. We saw several of these children change like a leaf on a tree, as soon as teacher and house-parents, according to our advice, entered into intimate conversation with these unhappy children.

This includes:

1. A continuous listening to the children, in order to 'seize' their utterances and to play the double part. As a result of this, the children open themselves more and more, because that behaviour has been reinforced. And this means that the children raise points of sometimes very deep feelings. They tell you everything, for instance, 'Why was mother crying when grandfather died?' 'Did you pray this morning?' 'For what?' 'We have no cross in our house' 'I don't like to go to church' 'Israelites are bad people' 'My mother did not pay in the shop, we had to leave suddenly'. If the teacher does not go into these subjects, he cannot hide his unintention reactions either. And this happens day by day.

2. A moving-up system. A mother-tongue cannot be taught by a different teacher every year. Therefore in our Institute, as in many, a teacher keeps his class as one family in deep friendship. The trust deaf children give to a good teacher, is enormous. It is almost as great as the trust they give to their parents.

3. The whole attitude of a good classroom teacher is *not* to be a subject-master. He is, on the contrary, involved in the total development of the child. As a human being and an educator he cannot but transfer his own ideals of life onto his children. He himself will become the model ('das Ich Ideal') – mainly unconsciously – to his children. So it is quite impossible to be a neutral teacher of the deaf. This is, in my opinion, contradictory.

We said that God is a vulnerable projection-screen, but that a falsification of His image can be corrected indirectly by educators other than the parents. Here too a teacher of the deaf has a specifically strong weapon in his trustworthiness and special intimacy with his pupils, against such falsifications. No teacher of other children has such powerful tools. But also a teacher and/or a house-parent can falsify the *image* of God, first of all by the atmosphere he creates in his group. A few examples:

Deaf children are rather inclined towards competition. It may be a temptation to some teacher to stimulate this unwisely for his didactic purposes. Such a teacher had better keep silent about God. It can be almost predicted that his pupils will imagine an exacting God, who rewards splendid achievements but not inner intentions.

Another example. A teacher or house-parent can play his part wrongly by discouraging his children: 'That is nonsense' 'You should not utter such stupidities!' 'Do you not understand that? But is is so easy! How stupid you are!' 'Don't say such silly things!' He may be too intellectual and have no eye nor appreciation for the childlike things his children produce and admire. He may show a kind of pride and a feeling of himself being far above his pupils. A teacher of this type, too, had better keep silent about God. He may prepare an image of a 'cavalier God'.

A direct influence
This is after all we have explained a matter of course. Because of his big influence he has to be very careful and should criticise himself/ herself continuously.

A teacher can mistakenly teach directly, Godly things, for instance, if he tells them that a baker can make bread, but not wheat. *God* makes wheat, flowers, plants, animals, water, sun, moon etc. *Men* make bread, houses, clothes etc. In this way he prepares an image of a 'God filling the gap'.

If the teacher introduces God's Omnipresence and Omniscience, as: 'Peter you go secretly into the kitchen. Mother has put the cookies

105

in the cupboard. Nobody is in the kitchen. Nobody can see you. You eat the cookies. But God is in the kitchen. God can see you . . .' etc. Proposed one sidedly the comforting truth of God's Omnipresence, an image of a 'police-God' is prepared by the teacher.

Undoubtedly a teacher of the deaf has an enormous influence upon his pupils, more so than with any other teacher of normal or handicapped children.

A real teacher of the deaf transfers to his children, consciously or unconsciously his views of life, his religion, his hopes and anxieties, his need and satisfactions, his ambitions and his memories, his whole way of reacting to persons and events, because all this is incarnated in teaching a mother-tongue. This is all foundation and outlook of many conscious and unconscious convictions and aspirations of his pupils, which hold for many years and appear almost unchangeable throughout their lives (Van Uden, 1968).

Our experience is – and I think every headmaster who has a survey over a series of classes and groups of deaf children, will agree that one can observe the character of the teacher within the behaviour of his pupils.

For instance there is a group of friendly, helpful children, who seldom quarrel or have difficulties. Look at the teacher. He or she is a real fatherly or motherly person.

But within another group, there are always quarrels. It seems to be a group of cocks and hens with quite a pecking hierarchy. Look at the teacher here. He/She imposes too much on them, playing them off against each other.

Another group might be clearly concientious, always in time, with nice manners, a little bit rigid . . . And the teacher? He is just the same.

I don't mention this as criticism of these devoted teachers. Not at all. These traits are at most 'les défauts de ses qualités'. I have my faults too. I tell this only to make clear how high the responsibility of a teacher of the deaf is towards his/her children.

CONCLUSION

When Jesus cured the blind man of Jericho, He said: 'Your faith has saved you' (Mc. 10.52). But when the father of a possessed epileptic child came to Jesus, he asked the faith not of that boy but of his father (Mc. 9. 23-24). In the same way when He cured the deaf mute, Jesus did not ask the faith from this speechless deaf man. So He asks

106

for *our* faith, the faith of the parents, of the educators, *for* the deaf children. *Our* faith will save them.

We have already said, that we have no choice between belief and disbelief, but only between one or another belief, this or that faith. The deaf will mainly have that faith, which *we* posses and which we transfer to him, consciously or unconsciously. May this stimulate us, to examine ourselves again, asking ourselves, whether our faith is pure and rich enough.

May our faith save our deaf by the grace of Christ!

SUMMARY

Human beings have a 'need to believe'. There is no choice between belief and disbelief. Our choice lies only between this or that belief. Consequently every teacher starts off from some belief. So do the parents. This process of believing takes place in deaf children too; Without help they come to some beliefs of the universe. The belief human beings develop spontaneously, is however in the main, wrong, i.e. full of egocentricity. The only belief, which does not encompass narrowness of mind, is that of charity even to our enemies, based on the love of our Father in Heaven. The healing value of this belief is authorised. – Religious education is to a great extent a process of preventing wrong beliefs in children by educating them in right beliefs. It is impossible for parents not to transfer to their children their – mainly unconscious – beliefs and pre-conceptions. This process is a symbiotic one and encloses body and mind by a world of conditionings and givings of meanings. This developmental process is described: how the parent-child relationship is projected in an image of God, formed by the child mainly unconsciously in the field of religion. God, however, is a very vulnerable projection-screen because His image, grown in our mind from early childhood, cannot be corrected easily, if it is wrong in some respect. – It is impossible for a teacher of the deaf not to transfer his beliefs to his children. It is explained, how the influence of a teacher of the deaf can be compared with that of the parents, because of the teaching of a mother-tongue by conversational methods. His influence is symbiotic too, direct but indirect also. He can correct or falsify the religious beliefs of his children. The responsibility of the teacher of the deaf is emphasised.

Question

If children at St. Michielsgestel are selected for the Oral School on the basis of their intelligence, could Fr. Van Uden please tell us what criteria govern his selection?

Answer

If the Performance IQ (Wechsler Intelligence Scale) is lower than 70, a pure oral way seems impossible. This means a *really* reliable IQ. It happens sometimes that a child, after a long period of educational neglect, scores very low in intelligence-testing. It is up to the ability of the psychologist to judge whether the score and profile are reliable. For instance we had a girl, the daughter of mentally defective parents, presented to our Institute at 7 years of age. Her first score was 69. After two years it was 81. After a further two years it was 93. A further four years and it was 115. This last figure was her reliable IQ.

Question

It has been said that the deaf are mainly 'copyists'. Does Fr. Van Uden feel that this is peculiar only to the deaf or does it not apply also to hearing people?

Answer

Every human being and especially a child is something of a monkey. Our integration into the culture of the environment is based on imitation and copying to a great extent. Look for example at the fashions for clothes coming from Paris. But a personality will conquer this dependency more and more by spontaneous creativity, one more, another less. It seems that there is a special danger that deaf children and adults stick too long in such copying and that they never conquer it sufficiently.

Question

If you, Father, were in a situation where combined communication was used in the out-of-school activities, what method would you use in the classroom?

Answer

My first reaction would be to send in my resignation, because the sight

108

day after day, in normal intelligent children, would be almost unbearable for me.

If that was however impossible, I would go into the playground myself and try to learn that esoteric language, make up lists of the signs used by the children and perhaps also film or video-record these sign-conversations. Then I would use that knowledge in the classroom, i.e. make the children more and more aware of the fact:

1. that one word or idiom can be expressed in more signs, for instance letter as phoneme and letter as written message;
2. that the signs have to be generalized, for instance that son is not only a baby but also an adult;
3. that there are shifts in meaning, for instance from the act of giving, to the gift or present, from 'a show' to 'to show', from transitivity to intransitivity as in 'to grow'.
4. that there is a transfer of meaning, for instance healthy for body-health, but also for food;
5. that there is a figurative meaning, for instance redeeming from a prison or slavery and redeeming from addictions;
6. that words can have flexions, which change the meanings, for instance single-plural and the belongings, for instance a friend's letter and a friendly letter.
7. that there are many words almost inexpressible in signs as 'relationship' *too* late' 'your friend *too*' etc.;
8. that different groupings of words can give different meanings, for instance 'the man we laughed at . . .' and 'we laughed at the man' etc.

So I would try to change the mixture language of the children into a 'co-ordinated bilingualism' (Osgood), i.e. that the children become more and more aware of two separated, distinguished languages: an oral one and a manual one. In this way I would first of all try to start *two* kinds of conversational lessons: pure oral lessons (with perhaps a lot of writing because lip-reading and speech will be too bad), and lessons using freely the 'gibberish' and translating it into normal language where misunderstandings are threatening. I would make the children aware of the many occasions and/or dangers of misunderstandings in their 'gibberish.'

I would try to bring them to *reading* as much as possible, and make them more and more aware of how reading is often disturbed by their of dehumanising, primitising and segregating effect of that 'gibberish',

'gibberish', e.g. a goods-train was understood as a 'good train' because of the sign for 'good.'

So I would try to work on the feelings and motivations of the children, to leave their signing more and more and go over to oral conversation even among themselves.

Last but not least, I would inform the parents; hand over to them the list of signs; – instruct them so that they have real conversations with their children in the same way as I have.

Question
If children are educated through oral methods in school, and at home the family uses gestures as a means of communication, what is the child's mother tongue?

Answer
We must distinguish between a family where all members are hearing, and a family where one or more members are deaf.

In the first case, there will not be a growth of sign-language. A language grows only within a group. The gestures (a gesture is not the same as a sign) will be no more than codes. In the family there will be no conversation between the deaf child and the hearing parents, which is a very bad situation and can evoke a deep emotional trauma. If the school is a good oral school, based on real conversation, the mother-tongue of that child will be that oral language. This lack of communication at home will not be based on the inability of the child but on the unacceptance by the parents.

If however there are more deaf members in that family, who converse by gestures and dramatisations, these gestures will become a sign-language as an esoteric language of that group.

This however can only happen when the school is a bad one and/or the deaf partner(s) is (are) unable to converse orally. If however the school is a good one, and the child is well integrated in that school, the oral language will certainly be his mother-tongue, but its growth to perfection will be hampered.

What is a bad oral school?

There are methods for the education of the deaf which incorporate too little of a real acceptance of the child's utterances. Understand me right! I don't blame anybody. Everything is meant well by those teachers, also with the child. But they are still forgetting something. Compare these two ways of working in a classroom of the deaf:

110

First Way of Working:
A picture is shown (an orchard)
Teacher: 'That is fruit. All say it . . .'
         'Where is the fruit John?'
John points to a tree.
Teacher: 'Yes the fruit is on the tree.'
         'Where is the fruit, Mary?'
Mary points to the basket; says: 'Basket.'
Teacher: 'Yes, all right! The fruit is in the basket. Everyone say it . . .'
         etc.

Second Way of Working:
A picture is shown (an orchard)
Teacher: 'Look, here is an orchard . . .' but at the same time he looks at the children, listening to what they have to say and how they express it . . . The children don't say anything yet, only look at the nice picture. John gesticulates and says something like: 'Home too! Worms thr'in . . . Bah!'
Teacher: 'John says: There was a worm in the fruit, Bah! . . . All say it!' . . . He writes it on the blackboard. 'Draw it John' . . . John does so, complete with worm!
Mary: 'Me too, eat, mouth . . . Bah!'
Teacher: 'You too? Say: I have had a worm in my mouth . . . Say it! . . .' The teacher writes it on the blackboard.
Teacher: 'Did you spit it out?'
Mary: 'Yes, Yes . . .' (acts it)
       All the children want to say something: Charles, that there are many worms in plums; Elly asks where the worms come from; Willy says that you have to watch for them in the shops etc., etc.

The teacher makes the right choice, he stimulates the *conversation*. It may be clear that this last way of working puts conversation, the playing of the double part, into the mid-point of the language acquisition. If the school does this in a pure oral way, it can be predicted that the oral language will be the children's mother-tongue, notwithstanding sometimes bad situations in the family. But we can be sure, that the parents, with only a little bit of acceptance of the child, will very soon experience that their child *is* able to converse with them.

Question
Do you, Father, use the written pattern to supplement the oral method?

Answer

Yes. This means that for normal deaf children a new word is taught 'from mouth to mouth' and *after* that it is written. So the written form is a complement to the spoken form, as a reinforcement. For example, *garage* is a new word. Some children will imitate it immediately without any written form. Suppose however some children do not, in which case the accentuated syllable is picked out: '*rage*'. After that '*ga-*' and then 'garage'. As soon as the child has spoken it, it is requested to write it down. This may be 'garaatsh', which phonetically is correct. The correct spelling must then be given to the child. It happens that it is necessary to pick one phoneme out, for instance *g*. 'Say gap . . .' The child says it. 'Now ga', etc. This procedure can be followed as early as the first grade. If the children cannot do so, then for instance 'raatsh' will be written by the teacher, but 'garaatsh' however 'from mouth to mouth'. Normal deaf children of 9 years of age in our school are able to imitate practically every new word by this procedure, the most difficult ones too. The same must be said about idioms and expressions, etc.

Question

To what extent does the movement of total communication effect our schools? Or is 'total communication' limited to the USA?

Answer

As far as I know, the theory of McCay Vernon on 'total communication' is still unknown in Europe. I do not know whether it is just limited to the USA. I hope so.

Question

Oral words are symbols for ideas. The meaning is fixed at first even with hearing children. For example there is another '*daddy*'. Every man is a daddy. Educational development *spreads* the meaning. This spread occurs equally whether the symbol be an oral or a manual one.

Answer

That word *equally* is to me incorrect. When the word 'daddy' is generalised, there is nothing in the word itself that hampers such a generalisation: it is an arbitary phonemic pattern. Let us suppose however that the child is using a sign for daddy, e.g. pointing to his right tooth, because daddy has a gold tooth: this sign will not so easily be generalised because it is concretely 'picturing'. The signs in sign-

112

language are mainly pictorial: this hampers transfer, abstraction and figurative meaning, etc. See Q. 3.

Question
Kindly explain the figures on page 38 with particular reference to 0 %.

Answer
'*All* deaf children' there includes the multiply handicapped. I have only an hypothesis why, in our research of 1971, the percentage of deaf children on the lowest level is zero. We have increasingly emphasised in these last few years the importance of reading. Furthermore the way of working on grammar became more and more reflective, which is based on reading. This too may have enhanced the reading at that age level. Besides this, we have given an ever-increasing amount of special help to our dysphasic deaf children, who usually are the worst readers.

Question
Briefly explain how you would introduce and explain an abstract e.g. *God* to a small deaf child.

Answer
I develop the idea of God in deaf children of about 8-9 years of age as follows:
I start from the continuous growing of things and the making-process of men. For example the making of bread. We take children into the bakery, or we try to make ourselves some bread in the school for domestic science. The process is symbolised as follows (fig. 1):
Who makes the wheat? *God.* I don't show pictures of God. I try to keep it mysterious. Who is God? Ooh, God is fine, God is good, God is dear. The same with other processes, e.g. the wooden chair, potatoes, clothes, lemonade, etc. Immediately the Omnipresence of God is taught by drawing a landscape and writing the name of God everywhere, with the help of the children, so that nothing is forgotten. Then we ask how many Gods now? Some children count, but almost always one or two hesitate. Then I continue 'No, not many, only one!' I write God in big letters so that the whole landscape is filled. This is extended outside the landscape 'Where do you live?' 'In Amsterdam'. 'Is God in Amsterdam?' 'Yes' . . . 'But God is not in Rotterdam!' Peter protests 'Yes!' almost angrily, 'Is God at home? Tell me where God is' etc.
Then the name *God* is written on the drawing mentioned above, on

the boy, on the sandwich, the bread, the flour, over the wheat . . . everywhere, and only one God (fig. 3 and 4).

Very soon we teach that God is our Father. The story of Jesus is especially used to show concretely how good God the Father is: God the Father lives in Jesus. Jesus is the Son of God the Father, etc.

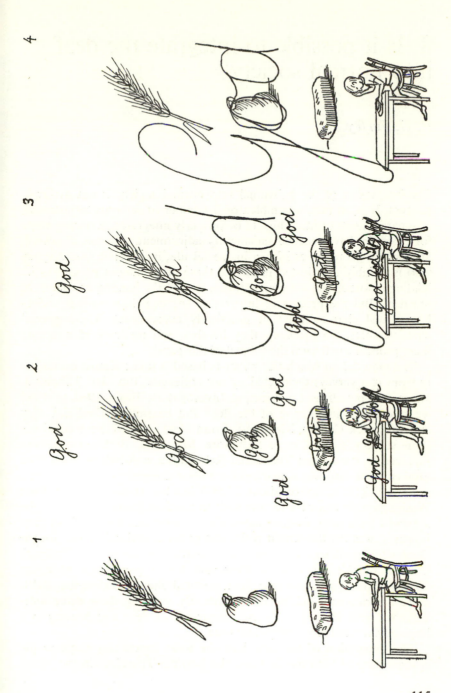

8. Is it possible to integrate the deaf into normal society?

P. H. Furfey

The integration of the individual into normal society is not a simple process. It is, in fact, a complex of a number of separate adjustments in separate areas of life. Thus, to be properly integrated, a person must, for example, have reached satisfactory adjustment at home, at school, at work, in his religious life, in his social life, in his civic life. Anyone who is notably unadjusted in any of these areas cannot be said to be leading a normal life. Of course this is true of the hearing as well as of the deaf. But the process of integrating the deaf into normal society has special characteristics at practically every point. These special characteristics, the problems they involve, and methods of attacking these problems will form the subject of this paper.

The material on which this paper is based is taken almost exclusively from two surveys conducted by my colleague, Rev. Dr. Thomas J. Harte and myself as Co-Principal Investigators. From 1962 to 1964 we studied the interaction of the deaf and hearing in Frederick City and Frederick County, Maryland. From 1964 to 1967 we studied the same subject in the City of Baltimore, Maryland. Both surveys were financed by the United Vocational Rehabilitation Administration. The total cost was just over a quarter of a million dollars.

Frederick is a city of about 22,000 located about 40 miles from Washington. It was easy for the staff to reach and small enough to be surveyed with some thoroughness. The greatest advantage of the city, however, was the fact that it is the seat of the Maryland School for the Deaf whose efficient staff was most helpful to our study. Frederick County, outside the City of Frederick has a population of about 50,000. Part of it is rich farm land, devoted chiefly to dairying. Baltimore has almost a million inhabitants. By studying these three locations we were able to study the interaction of deaf and hearing in a large city, a small city, and a rural area.

The integration of the deaf into the total community requires the co-operation of both the deaf and the hearing. Therefore in the Maryland surveys both the deaf and the hearing were studied. The principal technique for studying the deaf was the casework method. The first step was to locate the deaf. In Frederick City and County this did not prove difficult. There were stable communities where people tended to be widely acquainted. In the City of Frederick, 55 deaf persons were located; in the County, 25. In the large City of Baltimore the deaf were much harder to locate. All sorts of sources were used. The best sources proved to be schools for the deaf, deaf informants, societies for the deaf, and social agencies. Appeals were made over radio and television and advertisements were run in papers. By these various means, a grand total of 683 persons said to be deaf was located. Out of these a random sample of 155 was drawn for study. However, it was found that some supposed to be deaf were actually merely hard of hearing. The number of case studies actually made in Baltimore was 137.

Each deaf person and his family was normally visited twice. In addition, school records and court records were searched. Deaf persons in the sample who were still in school were observed there and their teachers were interviewed. There were regular case conferences at which the entire staff discussed each case and tried to interpret it. These were attended by an experienced caseworker who served as analyst.

The casework method was, as stated, the principal method used for studying the deaf. However, a number of special studies were undertaken to supplement this method, sometimes in Frederick, sometimes in Baltimore, sometimes in both places. One such study dealt with the shopping habits of the deaf. It was felt that information on this could better be obtained from the merchants than from the deaf themselves. Therefore in the Frederick survey, 291 retail merchants were selected, somewhat arbitrarily, as being the principal ones of the City and County. They were interviewed. About seveneights of them could recall having deaf customers and could give information about them. In both cities a study was made of manufacturers to find out whether they had had experience with deaf employees and what that experience had been. In Frederick, 23 manufacturers were located and all were interviewed. In Baltimore a stratified random sample of 136 out of 1514 manufacturers listed in the city was interviewed.

The case studies yielded some information about the religious life of the deaf; but it seemed desirable to question also the pastors of the deaf persons. Each was asked for his pastor's name. Then the latter was visited. In Frederick 37 clergymen were interviewed. In Baltimore the rectories of 25 Catholic parishes where deaf persons lived were visited and in all but one at least one priest was interviewed. There were also 12 interviews with non-Catholic clergymen. To obtain information about the health care of the deaf, a broad cross-section of health personnel was interviewed in Frederick. In Baltimore our group is now in the midst of a rather elaborate study of the health care of both the deaf and the blind.

Those who have contact with the deaf have often remarked on the special characteristics of deaf children of deaf parents. Such families are relatively rare. We could not depend on finding enough of them in our regular samples. Since the topic appeared interesting, it was decided to locate as many such families as we could and study them as a special group. In searching for these, we did not limit ourselves to Baltimore, but searched also in the surrounding county. Finally we located 11 deaf couples with a total of 20 deaf children.

The survey of the hearing involved structured interviews with a random sample of the hearing population, 18 years of age and over, of Frederick City and County and of the City of Baltimore. The design of the samples was rather complicated and need not be discussed here. It is worth remarking, however, that the analysis of results involved a great deal of calculation and would have been impossible were it not for the availability of the IBM electronic computer at Catholic University. The total number of interviews completed in Frederick City and County was 1017. In Baltimore it was 843.

The interviews schedule on which the structured interview was based consisted of five parts. One of these contained questions asking for social information about the interviews, such as sex, age, marital status, education and the like. The other parts of the schedule were designed to yield quantitative scores. They were: (1) Contact Score. This was a measure of the extent of the interviewee's contact with deaf persons. (2) Local knowledge Score. This part of the schedule was different in the Frederick and Baltimore surveys. It was designed to test the interviewee's knowledge concerning local facilities for the deaf (medical, educational, social-welfare). (3) General Knowledge Score. This was intended to measure information about the deaf and deafness in general. (4) Sociality. This score was obtained from the answers to two questions about the number of times the interviewee had gone out socially in the two weeks preceding the interview and the number of times he had received visitors into his home. The tests yielding these scores were carefully studied by techniques familiar to test psychologists and they were found to have surprisingly high reliabilities in view of their shortness.

118

It is now time to discuss our survey results insofar as they throw light on the integration of the deaf into normal society. I shall do this by discussing one by one the various adjustments the deaf person must make, the hurdles, so to speak, which he must pass over on his way to good adjustment.

The first step toward full integration is adjustment of the child to his home life. The importance of this can scarcely be overemphasized. An abnormal childhood makes later adjustment extremely difficult. In the vast majority of cases the parents of deaf children are hearing persons. For them the deaf child brings problems. First of all, they must grasp the fact that their child is deaf. This is not as easy as one might think. In at least three of our cases, the child was taken to a pediatrician who incorrectly assured the parents that he was not deaf. In one case the little girl was already five years old when this occurred.

After the child's deafness has been diagnosed, the parents must learn to accept the fact, to adjust to it emotionally. This is not always easy. Sometimes parents go from doctor to doctor in the vain hope of discovering a cure. Occasionally parents try bizarre expedients. One father took his deaf son on an airplane ride on the theory that reduced air pressure would somehow unstop the child's ears and make him hear.

Having accepted their child's handicap realistically, parents must then learn to give him the care he needs. Most of the parents in our study learned to do this. Some, however, tended to be overprotective. A teacher at a deaf school complained that one pupil would never do as well as he could because his parents were too lenient with him and never demanded that he do his best.

Outright parental rejection of a deaf child seems to be very rare indeed. However, some of the children were neglected on account of home circumstances. An overworked mother of a large family may not have the time and energy to give her deaf child the attention he needs. Extreme poverty makes life difficult for the deaf child as well as for the hearing. Some irregularity of family make-up, desertion, divorce, illegitimacy, may destroy the healthy emotional atmosphere which the child needs.

A deaf child, then, may be either overprotected or neglected by his hearing parents. It is pleasant to report, however, that in the majority of cases parents faced their responsibilities intelligently and faithfully. It is a somewhat remarkable fact that of the families with deaf child and hearing parents in the Frederick study, almost one-third moved to Frederick so that their children could attend the Maryland School for the Deaf. Other parents also went to a good deal of trouble to find the

119

best school for their child. Some learned signs and fingerspelling. Many went frequently to teachers for expert advice. In a word, in spite of frequent initial difficulties, most hearing parents learn to adjust.

A deaf child is fortunate if he is born to deaf parents. Such parents are normally quite disappointed that their child has been born deaf, but they are not overwhelmed. Moreover they know what to do. They teach the child to communicate by signs and later by fingerspelling. Therefore, the child is not isolated during his preschool years as the deaf child of hearing parents is likely to be. Perhaps the early stimulation of the deaf child by his deaf parents is intellectually stimulating. At least the following fact is suggestive. In our special study in Baltimore of deaf children of deaf parents, 20 such children were included. For 17 of these we had intelligence quotients and the mean of these was 111.5.

It may be appropriate to add a word here about families with hearing children and two deaf parents. There is one task that these parents cannot do very well. They cannot teach their children to talk. However, children associate with many others besides their parents and they usually learn to talk without difficulty. In communicating with their parents they most often use fingerspelling and conventional signs. One problem for these parents is that they cannot be informed by auditory cues when their young children are in distress. A hearing mother will respond if she hears her child in the next room start to cry. A deaf mother must keep visiting her child frequently if he is in another room or she must depend on some hearing person to help her.

If a deaf child is fortunate enough to be brought up in a happy, normal home he has passed the first hurdle on his way to integration into normal society. The second hurdle is the school. Specialized education is very necessary for the deaf and nearly all deaf children receive it. This specialized education is a very complex subject and the present report will not discuss it except to report on the social effects of two divergent systems for educating the deaf.

During the Frederick and Baltimore studies, the staff had close contact with two schools, the Maryland School for the Deaf (MSD), in Frederick and the William S. Baer (WSB) School in Baltimore, a school for handicapped children which had classes for the hearing-impaired. The former is a residential school; the latter, a day school. The WSB School used exclusively the oral method in communication. That is, the pupils were forbidden ever to use fingerspelling or conventional signs. They were to communicate solely through speech and lipreading. At MSD, on the other hand, the combined method was used. Every effort

120

was made to teach speech and lipreading; but the children were encouraged to use manual communication. In class teachers spoke and signed simultaneously.

As this audience knows, the dispute between the oralists and the proponents of the combined method is old and bitter. In the United States there seems to be almost no communication between the two groups. The oralists control the day schools which form parts of city school systems. The combined-method people control the state residential schools and also the two most advanced institutions for the deaf in the United States, Gallaudet College and the National Technical Institute for the Deaf.

The members of our staff were sociologists. As such, they were not concerned with educational techniques in themselves. But it did seem legitimate for them, as sociologists, to study the social consequences of the two contrasting systems of deaf education.

For the purpose of this study it was necessary to have some method of measuring hearing loss. It would have been ideal if audiometric data had been available for all our subjects. Unfortunately, they were not available for most adult subjects. Therefore, we used a simple substitute, the Gallaudet Hearing Scale (GHS), developed, as the name implies, at Gallaudet College. This scale consists of the following five questions which are asked the subject:

1. Can you hear loud noises?
2. Can you usually tell on kind of noise from another?
3. Can you usually tell the sound of speech from other sounds?
4. Can you usually hear and understand a few words without seeing the speaker's face and lips?
5. Can you usually hear and understand most of the things a person says to you without seeing his face and lips?

The score of the GHS is the number of questions answered affirmatively. Scores obviously can run from 0 to 5. GHS has been compared with audiometric results and for such a short scale it does remarkably well. It seems entirely satisfactory for group comparisons such as were used in our study.

To measure the communication ability of the deaf, two rating scales were used, one to measure ability to communicate with other deaf persons and one to measure ability to communicate with the hearing. Both were five-point scales, the highest rating being 'Excellent' and the lowest being 'None or Practically None'.

The deaf subjects in the Baltmore survey had been educated at quite

121

a variety of schools. To simplify matters, it was decided to limit the comparison to two groups: (1) those educated exclusively at the WSB School or this school and other oral schools, and (2) those educated exclusively at MSD or at MSD and other combined-method schools. Table 1 shows the results of the comparison.

Table 1. *Hearing level and communication ability by type of school.*

School	Mean GHS	Mean Communication Score Hearing	Mean Communication Score Deaf
WSB or WSB and Other Oral Schools	2.32	2.84	1.76
MSD or MSD and Other Combined Method Schools	1.13	2.96	3.04

The table shows that the MSD students were very much better in their ability to communicate with the deaf. This is not surprising. For communication among the deaf is nearly always manual and practice in such communication is forbidden at oral schools. The other principal finding is, however, a bit astonishing. Although the hearing loss of the MSD students was markedly greater than the hearing loss of those educated in oral schools, the MSD alumni were a bit better in communicating with the hearing. This fact seems to refute the principal argument of the oralists. They claim that by forbidding their pupils to communicate manually, they force them to concentrate on oral communication. Our evidence shows that this concentration failed to bring the expected results.

Certainly all deaf persons should be taught manual communication. Of course they should also be taught speech and lipreading; but these are no substitute for signing. First of all, not all deaf persons, not even all very intelligent deaf persons, can learn to lipread. Lipreading can be very useful under certain circumstances, but it cannot wholly supplant oral communication. The deaf who cannot sign and fingerspell are very much handicapped under some circumstances. When they attend an oral school they may fail to learn because they simply cannot follow the teacher. They cannot participate in religious services. They are cut off from social life with the other deaf. It is important that the deaf should be able to get together socially. In the Baltimore survey seven deaf girls were found who had been seduced by hearing men. No case of seduction by a deaf man was found.

A third adjustment which a deaf person must make to be integrated

122

into normal society is the economic adjustment. That is, the person must be economically self-sufficient. This generally means being a wage earner or a housewife. Information on employment comes in our survey from two sources, the case studies and the special surveys of manufacturers.

Both the Frederick and the Baltimore surveys showed the deaf to be steady workers. In neither city were there any adult deaf who were 'unemployed' in the technical sense of being without a job and looking for a job. The adult deaf who were not working were 'not in the labor force' for various reasons. Some were housewives, students, or retirees. Some were prevented from working by a physical handicap; but interestingly enough, the handicap was always something other than deafness.

The range of occupations open to the deaf is, of course, limited. Some jobs are closed to them because they essentially involve communication with the public; such jobs, for example, as telephone operator or salesman. Some jobs are unsuitable because they are not routine, but require frequent oral instruction from a foreman. Sometimes a machine operator must monitor his machine by ear. He can tell by the sound if it is not operating properly. Finally, as one plant manager said, 'Hearing is a safety device', and the deaf cannot be employed in some dangerous factory situations because they lack the hearing to warn them of approaching danger.

There remain, however, a rather wide variety of occupations at which the deaf can, and do, work very satisfactorily. In the United States the most common professional occupation is teacher in a school for the deaf. The most common skilled workers are those in the printing trades. In the present survey the occupations of the deaf were not typical. In Frederick the average occupational status of the deaf was above average because 12 of the 54 employed deaf were teachers at MSD. In Baltimore, on the other hand, the status tended to be low. This was due to the presence of a large proportion of non-whites. Racial prejudice made it hard for the Negro deaf to get good jobs. Of this, more later.

The most interesting result of the survey of manufacturers was the high ratings given the deaf as workers. At each plant, two persons were asked to rate deaf workers in comparison with hearing workers holding the same job. The two raters were the personnel manager or other person responsible for hiring and firing, and the foreman in immediate charge of a deaf worker. The personnel managers rated the deaf as better than average. However, the foreman who had the opportunity to

123

observe his deaf worker day by day, rated the deaf much better. Of 130 ratings only one rated the deaf as 'a little below average'. The others rated the deaf as being as good as, or better than, hearing workers.

It would seem from the survey that the deaf have excellent economic potential. There is reason to hope that the new fair-employment laws will eliminate the effect of racial discrimination. There remains, however, one problem. There is need for more opportunities for vocational education. The Baltimore public-school system offers no special vocational training for the deaf. The deaf pupils who attend vocational classes geared to the hearing will not learn much. Pupils at MSD have excellent opportunities; but these opportunities should be universal.

The young deaf child must learn to adjust to life in his parental family. When he grows up he probably marries and then he must learn to adjust to family life in a family of his own. The first kind of adjustment has already been discussed; now we shall discuss the second type, particularly adjustment as a spouse. Most of the relevant data come from the Baltimore survey.

Three types of marriages involving a deaf person may be distinguished. One is the marriage in which both husband and wife are deaf. This we call a 'deaf-deaf marriage'. Then there is the mixed deaf-hearing marriage in which the husband is deaf. Finally there is the mixed marriage in which the wife is deaf.

In the principal Baltimore sample, there were 21 deaf-deaf couples as well as three widows and one widower who were surviving spouses of such marriages. As far as our evidence goes, all these marriages seemed stable. However, there was evidence that three of the present spouses in deaf-deaf marriages had been unsuccessful in such marriages in the past. There had been two divorces and one annulment. However, in all three cases, there had been a remarriage to a deaf person and these three couples are among our present 21 deaf-deaf couples.

The sample contains five mixed marriages with deaf husband. All five seem stable now. However, in the past one couple had two temporary separations. One couple has a certain amount of husband-wife friction; but it is nevertheless rated stable by our caseworker. Interestingly, the wife states that she feels she could clear up this little friction if she could talk it over with her husband; he, however, is very poor in communicating with the hearing.

The 15 cases in the sample of mixed marriages with deaf wife contrast with the perceding types by their great instability. Seven were rated stable. These include 4 marriages in which the husband is now

124

dead. Two of the remaining marriages are rated as probably stable; but the remaining six are rated as definite failures. It seems true that hearing husbands often make poor spouses for deaf wives. In this connection, it is worth recalling what was said previously. Deaf girls are sometimes seduced by hearing men; but in our sample we found no cases of seduction by deaf men. There seems to be a moral to this. Should not Catholic educators of the deaf try hard to provide opportunities for deaf girls to meet deaf men?

Of course the most important adjustment a deaf person (or anyone else) must make is the religious adjustment. Since I am speaking to an audience of experts on the subject, I shall not presume to discuss the religious life of the deaf. I shall, however, mention one extremely significant fact that turned up in the course of the survey. In both Frederick and Baltimore the attempt was made to interview the clergy who staffed the churches which the deaf attended. In Frederick only 6 of the 37 clergymen interviewed were aware of the deaf members of their congregations. In Baltimore priests at 24 parishes were seen. At 5 parishes a priest knew personally all the deaf of the parish. At 2, the priest knew some, but not all. At 4 he knew the deaf by hearsay. At 3 he knew the deaf persons, but did not know they were deaf. However, there were 10 parishes in which the priests were totally unaware of their deaf parishioners. Twelve non-Catholic clergymen were also interviewed in Baltimore. Of these, 9 knew, directly or indirectly, that they had deaf members in their congregations, 2 did not, and 1 did not know that the person in question was deaf. The Baltimore showing seems to be better than Frederick. Perhaps this is because there is a full-time priest, a full-time minister, and a part-time minister assigned to work with the Baltimore deaf. The conclusion to which these facts point is clear. The religious life of the deaf will be sadly neglected unless specially trained personnel is assigned to the work.

Integration into society demands a normal social life for the participant. Since only the very exceptional deaf person can read lips well enough to socialize very well with the hearing, most of the social life of the deaf takes place with each other where communication is manual. To facilitate this, a great many clubs have been organized. Some are general social clubs. Some are special-purpose groups, such as athletic clubs. Clubs exist on the local, statewide, national and even international level. Where special religious services for the deaf are held, there is usually at least an informal get-together afterwards and this is more or less equivalent to a club.

In Frederick about two thirds of the adult deaf belonged to clubs. In

125

Baltimore the proportion was about one-third. The reason for this difference is not entirely clear. Perhaps it is easier to get together in the small-city atmosphere of Frederick. The proportion of nonwhite deaf was higher in Baltimore and, although they were not formally excluded from the deaf clubs, it may be that they felt less than completely welcome.

Social clubs seem to play an important role in the lives of many deaf persons. Some in both the Frederick and the Baltimore sample belonged to three of four such clubs. Yet a considerable fraction do not belong. Why is this? Partly it may be due to isolation. A person living in a remote rural area cannot easily get to the meetings. Then there is psychological isolation. Some persons are less sociable than others. Then there are doubtless some who have found other forms of social life besides the social life of the club. The automobile has made social visiting easier. Even a small circle of close friends and relatives may provide a very satisfactory social life. All in all, it would seem that the deaf are more dependent on clubs for their socializing, but they are not entirely dependent on clubs.

To be integrated into normal society, one must obviously be a law-abiding citizen. In this respect, the deaf seem to do rather well. Among the 80 Frederick deaf there were no arrests of adults nor were there any cases of juvenile delinquency. In Baltimore, among the 137 persons in the sample, police records showed that 8 persons had been arrested a total of 14 times. Of the 14 arrests, 10 were for disorderly conduct, 3 for assault, and 1 for larceny. No offender was imprisoned, although one was committed to a psychiatric institution for observation. Fines ($ 5 and costs to $ 50 and costs), suspended sentences, and probation were the usual dispositions of the cases.

All the state penal institutions in Maryland were visited by a staff member and the principal officials were interviewed. The process did not turn up much information. No records were kept distinguishing deaf from hearing prisoners. The recollections of prison officials were usually quite vague. Only one deaf prisoner was found actually present in the institutions visited.

One gets the impression that the crime rate is lower among the deaf than among the hearing. If this is true, one reason may be that many crimes require speech and hearing. Another interesting fact is that police officials interviewed in Baltimore stated that police were reluctant to arrest the deaf.

In the Frederick study there were half a dozen cases of deaf women who either bore illegitimate children or were known to the police for keeping bad company. In the Baltimore study nine deaf women were found who had been pregnant out of wedlock at one time or another. One of the nine was a 16-year old girl. Of the remaining 8, there were 7 who ultimately married. Marital adjustment was not perfect in every case; but at least no one became a criminal or a prostitute. No one is under police surveillance.

The health care of the deaf involves special problems; and there are few persons among health personnel who are equipped to solve these problems. An essential part of a good medical examination is the taking of a health history. If the physician must rely on paper and pencil or on an interpreter there is a danger that the history may not be sufficiently thorough. It is hard for the physician to give instructions that will be well understood and to answer the patient's questions. The same difficulties recur in the nurse-patient relationship. Nurses probably gave adequate physical care; where they fell down was in dealing with the patient's psychology. The Frederick report states: 'No nurse felt is was her responsibility to prepare the deaf patient for the usual and unusual hospital routine. No nurse felt it was her place to assist the deaf patient to work through his anxiety'.

Neither the Frederick nor the Baltimore survey covered social work and the deaf; so one can only speculate about the subject. However, our workers did find, particularly in Baltimore, some families of the deaf who were living in extreme poverty and who were extremely disorganized. Social workers are trained to help families overcome such unfavorable conditions. However, it is doubtful whether, either in Frederick or Baltimore, deaf families received any but the very simplest forms of help from social agencies.

A few words will be added here about the survey of the deaf as shoppers made by questioning the retail merchants in the Frederick survey. The vast majority of the merchants were familiar with deaf customers. Their general impression was favorable. They tended to believe that 'the deaf are somewhat more friendly than the hearing, that they are somewhat easier to please, are somewhat wiser spenders, and probably a bit more sensitive'. Shopping seems to present no great problem to the deaf.

Thus far this paper has discussed the integration into society of what one might call the 'normal' deaf, that is, those in whom deafness is the only serious disability. However, there are some groups of persons for whom this is not true. They have some additional disability. In such cases it sometimes happens that the person would be able to adjust in spite of deafness alone or in spite of the other disability alone;

but the combination of two disabilities is too much for him.

When deafness is due, not to heredity, but to some condition affecting the central nervous system, the person is likely to show some other physical handicap in addition to deafness; he is a 'multiply handicapped' person. In the Baltimore sample there were 17 schoolchildren or recent school graduates for whom sufficiently complete clinical records were available to identify them as multiply handicapped. Of the most serious among these cases, the clinical record states that 'his hyperkinetic, disorganized, poorly goaldirected behavior is characteristic of the child with organic brain damaga'. This child's behavior was so abnormal that he could not remain at home; he was institutionalized at the age of ten. On the other hand there were some with only mild physical symptoms in addition to deafness and the hope seemed good that they could adjust to normal life.

Many of the multiply handicapped – as well as some other – deaf suffer from mental retardation. The possibility that a retarded deaf child can be integrated into normal society depends, of course, on the seriousness of his retardation. It depends, too, on the availability of appropriate vocational education. A retarded child needs a great deal of care and attention to help him adjust. Communication difficulties make it harder to give this care and attention in the case of a deaf child.

It is an embarrassing fact – but it is a fact that must be faced – that in the United States nonwhites suffer from discrimination. To be both black and deaf is therefore a sort of multiple handicap. In the Frederick survey only 4 nonwhites were found and one cannot generalize from so few. In the Baltimore sample there were 37, of whom 35 were Negroes and 2 were Indians. What follows refers to the nonwhites in Baltimore. Until rather recently the Baltimore school system was segregated. When this is the case, Negro schools almost inevitably suffer. It is not surprising, then, that twice as many whites as nonwhites were high-school graduates. Whites far excelled nonwhites in communication skills with both the hearing and the deaf; this also is an index of differences in quality of education. Opportunities for vocational education for the nonwhite deaf have been very poor in the past. This fact is reflected in the finding that 14% of the nonwhites were unskilled workers as against 3% of the whites. The staff rated 14% of the whites as being below average in economic status; for nonwhites the figure was 41%. Let us hope that the present drive against discrimination in America will radically improve the lot of the nonwhite deaf.

Sometimes it happens that a special set of circumstances or a particular psychological quirk tends to isolate a person and cut him off to

128

a greater or less extent from his fellow men. This danger of isolation may be looked on as a sort of handicap which most people can successfully overcome. However, a deaf person finds it harder to overcome. In the Baltimore survey the staff paid particular attention to isolation and found several instances varying from mild to severe. A mild case is that of an unmarried woman in her early sixties who lives alone and works at a semi-skilled job. If she were a hearing woman, she would probably strike up an acquaintance with neighbours, gossip with the corner storekeeper, and so on. But she is deaf. Of course, she could join a deaf club, but she does not care to take the trouble. Inevitably, the result is a certain isolation. An extreme case is a Negro man in his fifties who lives with his sister who works as a maid. He has no communication skills beyond natural gestures such as pointing to communicate with his sister. He spends most of his time simply wandering around aimlessly.

The survey of the hearing brought some interesting results. One of the most interesting findings was the small amount of social contact between the deaf and the hearing. You will remember that interviewees were tested by questions yielding a Contact Score. Principally this test consisted in asking interviewees whether they had, at present or in the past, any deaf neighbours, deaf fellow-employees, deaf fellow church members, and so on. Note that the mere presence of a deaf person in the same social group as the interviewee was enough to yield a positive score. They did not need to be friends. If the interviewee and the deaf person were at present members of the same group the score was 2; if it was only in the past the score was 1. Suppose, then, that all an interviewee could remember about social contact with the deaf was that he knew that a deaf couple used once to live down the block. Such a person would be given a Contact Score of 1. The mean Contact Score for the whole Baltimore survey was only 1.15, only a tiny fraction more than the hypothetical man just mentioned. The average score was higher in Frederick City, 2.42 which is scarcely surprising in view of the presence of MSD there. In Frederick County, City excluded, it was 1.45.

Mean Contact Scores were higher for men than for women and higher for whites than for nonwhites. This probably means that men get around more than women and meet more people, therefore also more deaf people. The same is probably true of nonwhites. Their social world is restricted both in Frederick and in Baltimore.

You will remember that interviewees were also tested on General Knowledge of deafness and the deaf as well on the Local Knowledge cf local conditions. The two scores correlated with each other and with Contact Score. The correlations were too high to be explained by chance, but they were nevertheless rather low. There were differences between occupational groups on both the Local and General Knowledge Scores. The professional and managerial group came first, followed in order by the clerical and sales group, and the skilled workers. Education showed only slight correlation with the knowledge scores and age correlated negatively with them.

Let me conclude this paper with a few words on the general thrust of the Frederick and Baltimore surveys. This paper has been an attempt to answer a Question, 'Is it possible to integrate the deaf into normal society?' The answer is an unhesitating 'yes'. It is being done all the time. Of course some deaf cannot be so integrated, just as some hearing persons cannot be. But the average, run-of-the-mill deaf person is being integrated and is living a normal, healthy, useful life.

However, all this does not happen automatically. Our survey strongly emphasized what we suspected all along. The deaf need treatment at every point. The deaf schoolchild needs a special kind of school. The deaf need a special kind of vocational training. Children and parents in deaf families have special problems which they must meet in special ways. The deaf need special medical care. And so on.

Actually, in the United States, the deaf are receiving a great deal of special aid in one way or another; but still more is needed. A special difficulty is the invisibility of the deaf. The survey results just quoted show that the average citizen has remarkably little contact with the deaf. This being the case, it is not surprising that there is not more public discussion of the needs of the deaf. Possibly we who are professionally concerned with the deaf in one way or another should give a bit more of our time to the hearing. They need education.

QUESTIONS

1. Concerning your table on page 122. As far as I can see, these figures are based on subjective ratings. Why did you not use a test *in addition* to the answers of these ratings, to be quite sure, that the results are not the effect of a subjective set? My objection is as follows:
These children of the oral schools had more hearing than those of

the deaf school(s), even in such a degree that they were in my opinion on the average, not deaf in the strict sense of that word. If one can 'tell one kind of noise from another', one can hear his own voice while speaking which immediately gives a better impression of one's speech, even if not understood. If one has to judge the communication of such a person, one may *expect* a higher intelligibility which is frustrated, and the judgment will be lower on a subjective basis. If on the other side one hears a deaf voice, one may expect a bad intelligibility, but the judgment on the scale can be enhanced because of better understanding than expected. I suspect that the figures for 'mean communication score hearing' have been influenced by these sets and do not mirror objective proportions. You know the research of Quigley and Frisina (Frisina 1963) who found a significantly better lipreading of deaf children in a hearing environment than a control group of deaf children in a combined environment.

2. You do not mention the achievement level, most of all the reading level, of your deaf subjects. The results of reading tests in the u.s. (1962, 1969, see my paper) are very dissatisfying for both oral and combined schools. Communication with the hearing is not only dependent upon oralism or manualism but also on the content of communication.

a. *Content* cannot be anywhere but at a low standard if the person cannot read and is almost illiterate. This may be a reason of low standard communication with the hearing.

b. This illiteracy has a *levelling* effect on the deaf: they almost all (more than 90%) have the same low standard of cultural achievement.

The results of your study that the deaf have almost no entertainment with the hearing and are almost totally dependent on the deaf club for their social entertainment, may be the effect of that low achievement standard.

As soon as you have deaf subjects who can read, there occurs a kind of dissolution of deaf clubs. This is the experience we have in our country. There is a lot of really good entertainment of our deaf alumni and the hearing. The entertainment for the deaf however is mainly not based on deaf *clubs,* but on intimate encounters in their own homes in very small groups of personal friendships, mostly according to their achievement levels. To give you some figures of the alumni of our school (1971):
1270 alumni
Unmarried: 668 = 52,6 %

Married: 573 = 47,4 %
235 couples, both deaf persons: 78 %
118 couples, males or females hearing: 22 %
Data of Rev. Ad. van Beers, dept. Aftercare St. Michielsgestel.

3. Page 7 you say: 'A deaf child is fortunate if he is born to deaf parents'. This is not in agreement with the results of research in our Institute (see my first paper); the deaf children of deaf parents – in general deaf children of families where there are more than one deaf person – appeared to be more aggressive than the other ones. I suspect that the difficulties of deaf children with their hearing parents mentioned by you, are based on a too low average standard of achievement.

4. Why did you not analyse the manual conversation of at least a sample of deaf persons?
  Tervoort (1953) analysed such a conversation. The results show a lot of misunderstandings as soon as the partners leave the present concrete level of the content of their conversation. I don't think that the manual conversation of your subjects is any better. The effect of such a conversation shown to an outsider who is not aware of its content, is, that it looks very lively. That vividness however does not seem to be mainly the effect of a good conversation but is exactly the opposite. They repeat and repeat in a more and more lively style in order to bring their thoughts to the other, who still does not understand and gives wrong answers and so forth.
  I refer to the research of Myklebust (1964) who found in students of Gallaudet College a pseudo-hypomanic behaviour which to him can be explained (in combination with extraversion and pseudo-schizoid behaviour, acc. to MMPI) by feelings of desolation notwithstanding a deaf environment in that college.

ANSWER

I deeply appreciate the courtesy of Father van Uden in allowing me to respond to the questions which he raised concerning my paper. I shall try to discuss all his comments, although, for the sake of convenience, my reponses will not follow precisely the same order as his questions.
  The reader will remember that Father Harte and I studied a random sample of the alumni of two schools who were living in Baltimore at the time. One school used the pure oral method (speech and speech-

reading only) whereas the other used the combined method (speech and speechreading plus fingerspelling and signs). We felt that both schools were excellent representatives of the two educational systems. By using the Gallaudet Hearing Scale, we found that the alumni of the combined-method school had a very much greater average hearing loss than the alumni of the other school. However, in spite of this fact, the combined-method alumni did as well, in fact slightly, but not significantly, better than the oral-method alumni in communicating with the hearing; and of course they did enormously better in communicating with the deaf.

Father van Uden objects that our results were based on 'subjective' ratings and asks why we did not use tests in addition. The reason is purely practical. Our subjects were adults scattered throughout a large city. It just would not be feasible to round up such people and subject them to audiometry and elaborate paper-and-pencil tests. However, the Gallaudet Hearing Scale which we used is known to be a valid test.[1] Also, it seems to be rather simple for a hearing person to judge how well a deaf person can communicate with him. Our results were very clear-cut and definite. I do not think that many impartial experts would question them.

However, our study does not stand alone. There are a growing number of objective studies comparing deaf children of deaf parents with deaf children of hearing parents. Children in the former group were taught manual communication from infancy; children in the latter group were not. It is astounding that in *every* case where a significant difference was found, it was in favor of the manual group. Thus Brill found that deaf children of deaf parents had higher IQ's.[2] Goetzinger and Rousey,[3] Denton,[4] and Maffeo[5] found they had higher test scores on academic subjects. Stevenson found that 90 per cent of them were better students and attained a higher educational level than the paired children of hearing parents.[6] Meadows proved that they were superior not only in school work, but also in personal adjustment.[7] Stuckless and Birch found superiority in communication skills including, in this case, even speechreading.[8] Vernon and Kohl discovered no difference between the two groups in communication, but the school work of the manual children was superior.[9] Montgomery found no negative correlation between oral skills and manual communication.[10] Father Harte and I made no study of the type just discussed; but we did make case studies of all the deaf children of deaf parents whom we could find. We found 20; of these we were able to get IQ's for 17. The average was 111.5, which seems extraordinarily high.

133

A number of other studies point in the same general direction. House and Fitch compared two groups of deaf children of hearing parents; in one group the hearing parents had studied manual communication, whereas the other group had not.[11] The number of cases (4 pairs) was too small to yield significant differences; however, the approach is promising. As the reader doubtless knows, the Rochester method is a compromise between the pure oral and the combined method. It teaches speech, speechreading and fingerspelling, but excludes signs. It is therefore a *partly* combined method. Hester,[12] Klopping,[13] and Quigley[14] compared the results of the Rochester method to the results of pure oralism. In general, the Rochester method proved superior, but the results were less striking than those of the preceding paragraph. Apparently, even a restricted use of manual communication is beneficial, but not as beneficial as its unrestricted use.

Father van Uden quotes a study that might seem at first sight to be slightly inconsistent with the results just discussed. He mentions Quigley and Frisina (Frisina 1963) as finding 'a significantly better lipreading of deaf children in a hearing environment than a control group of deaf children in a combined environment.' Since Father van Uden does not give an exact reference, it is hard to check back. I have one Quigley and Frisina reference.[15] However, this piece of research seems totally irrelevant to the present topic. It compares resident students with day students of schools for the deaf. Both groups were receiving the same sort of education in school. The study has no relevance for the comparison of pure oralism versus the combined method. Of course the day students, as Father van Uden says, did have a greater exposure to a hearing environment. They proved, as he says, superior in lipreading. They were also superior in speech. On the other hand the day students seemed somewhat inferior in psycho-social adjustment.

Let me mention here that the brevity of Father van Uden's references makes it difficult for me to identify them and therefore difficult to comment on them fairly. He cites Tervoort (1963) and Myklebust (1964) for certain opinions unfavorable to manual communication. If I guess correctly what he is referring to,[16] I cannot see that they have the meanings Father van Uden ascribes to them. However, it may be that I have not found the correct references.

Is it not time to recognize frankly that it is impossible to attain the objective of the pure oralists, as often stated by its proponents, that is, to establish the deaf as full and regular members of hearing society? Father Harte and I found plenty of evidence that this is, indeed, impossible. The 137 persons in our random sample of the Baltimore deaf

134

were rated by our staff on their ability to communicate with the hearing. Among them, 27 were rated 'excellent.' However, the reader must remember that this means 'excellent as compared to the average deaf person.' This is, indeed, a modest degree of communication. The most skillful speechreader can neither read speech in the dark nor in a dim light nor when the speaker's back is turned nor when the speaker is at some distance. He cannot understand what is said over a loudspeaker or the radio. Even under ideal conditions, he must rely largely on guesswork because a great many speech sounds cannot be distinguished by watching the speaker's face.

The degree of communication of the deaf with the hearing which Father Harte and I defined as 'excellent' is thus – realistically – very modest indeed. Yet only 21 of our 137 subjects attained this degree of communication. What is very striking is that 15 out of these 21 became deaf after learning to speak and all the remaining 6, though post-linguistically deaf, had a considerable degree of residual hearing. It is interesting to note that only about a third of these 'excellent' communicators had ever gone to a school for the deaf, about half to oral and half to combined-method schools. Thus neither method can claim much credit for the success of these communicators.

Of course practically everyone agrees that every effort should be made to teach the deaf child speech and speechreading to the full limit of his ability. Even a little ability to communicate with the hearing is useful, just as a modest smattering of a foreign language can be very helpful to the visitor to a foreign country. It can be helpful in shopping, in asking directions, in making courteous replies to friendly overtures. However, this sphere of usefulness is obviously very limited.

A prelinguistically deaf child who is also profoundly deaf can, as has been seen, learn to communicate with the hearing only to a modest degree. If he is prevented by his oralist teachers from learning manual communication, then he becomes a social isolate. This is a deplorable fate. Father Harte and I found more than a few such tragic cases in our Baltimore study.

Father van Uden has a most surprising idea of the nature of manual communication. He believes that those who communicate manually 'repeat and repeat in a more and more lively style in order to bring their thoughts to the other, who still does not understand and gives wrong answers and so forth.' Recently professional linguists have been studying the language of signs and their findings flatly contradict Father van Uden's impressions. What these linguists have found is succinctly stated by Bergman who writes that American Sign Language, as he calls it, 'represents a precise and rapid medium of communication capable of expressing abstractions, nuances of meaning, and sparkling witticisms, and is a living and growing language as well.'[17] The language of signs is, indeed, the natural language of the profoundly deaf child. If he attains some skill in speech and speechreading, this is to him a second language, in which he is never quite at home.

If the findings of the linguists seem too theoretical to impress the ordinary reader, he has only to look at concrete results. Take Gallaudet College as an example. This institution uses the combined method. Teachers speak, fingerspell, and sign at the same time. However, students depend principally on manual communication. If they could hear well enough to understand a lecture, there would hardly be a reason for going to Gallaudet. Yet for over a century college subjects have been taught successfully there. There is even a graduate program. And what started so successfully at Gallaudet is spreading to other American institutions. All sorts of difficult and abstract subjects have been taught manually with success up to the limit of the student's intellectual ability.

Manual communication makes club life possible for the deaf. However, I am afraid Father van Uden misinterpreted our results when he states that we found that the deaf 'are almost totally dependent on the deaf club for their social entertainment.' Actually, we found that 63.5 per cent of the deaf in our sample did not belong to any club. For a minority, however, a deaf club played a very important role in their social life.

Manual communication was more important in the religious life of the deaf. An important finding of our study was that in all denominations the deaf were almost totally neglected, except where some clergyman was particularly assigned to work with the deaf. This means a clergyman who could communicate manually. In a large church even the best speechreader is not likely to understand much of what is said in the pulpit or at the altar. Manual communication makes common worship possible.

To me, perhaps the most surprising opinion expressed by Father van Uden is to the effect that 'sign language' is not a good vehicle for religious education because manual communication is too concrete. 'Sign language is mainly a "picture-language".' I am not sure that religious instruction should be abstract. The parables of the New Testament seem to me to be very concrete, even a sort of 'picture-language.' However, if religion is to be taught, partly at least, in abstract terms, this should not prove too difficult. It should not be harder than the teaching of college subjects on the abstract level, and this has proved

136

altogether feasible at colleges for the deaf where manual communication is used.

In conclusion may I emphasize something that seems to me quite evident? Modern research has very convincingly shown the superiority of the combined method over pure oralism. The traditional fear that manual communication would divert the pupil from the study of speech has proved altogether groundless. In fact, just the opposite of what the oralists feared has proved to be the case. The combined method has proved more efficient in the teaching of speech and speechreading, just as it has proved more efficient in the teaching of other subjects. And on the other hand the oralists' traditional policy of discouraging manual communication has resulted in cases of very tragic social isolation, children who could not learn to communicate orally and who were forbidden to communicate manually. I hope that all educators of the deaf will have the courage to face these facts. A great deal is at stake.

NOTES TO MR. FURFEY'S ANSWER

1. Jerome D. Schein, *The Deaf Community Study of Washington, D.C. I. Methodological Report* (Washington: Gallaudet College, 1964).
2. Richard C. Brill, 'The Superior I.Q.'s of Deaf Children of Deaf Parents', *Maryland Bulletin*, 90: 97-98, 110-111, 1970.
3. C. P. Goetzinger and C. L. Rousey, 'Educational Development of Deaf Children', *Amer. Annals of the Deaf*, 104: 221-31, 1959.
4. David M. Denton, 'A Study of the Educational Achievement of Deaf Children (a Survey)' in *Report of the Proceedings of the Forty-Second Meeting of the Convention of American Instructors of the Deaf* (Washington: Government Printing Office, 1966), pp. 428-38.
5. Carla E. Maffeo, 'The Effect of Pre-school Manual Communication on the Academic Development of Deaf Children'. Unpublished manuscript, Bureau of Social Research, Catholic University of America, 1972.
6. Elwood A. Stevenson, 'A Study of the Educational Achievement of Deaf Children of Deaf Parents', *California News*, September, 1964, pp. 1-3.
7. Kathryn P. Meadows, 'Early Manual Communication in Relation to the Deaf Child's Intellectual, Social, and Communicating Function', *Amer. Annals of the Deaf*, 113: 29-41, 1968.
8. E. R. Stuckless and J. W. Birch, 'The Influence of Early Manual Communication on the Linguistic Development of Deaf Children', *Amer. Annals of the Deaf*, 111: 452-60, 1966.
9. McCay Vernon and S. D. Kohl, 'Early Manual Communication and Deaf Children's Achievement', *Amer. Annals of the Deaf*, 115: 527-36, 1970.
10. G. W. G. Montgomery, 'The Relationship of Oral Skills to Manual Communication in Profoundly Deaf Adolescents', *Amer. Annals of the Deaf*, 11: 557-65, 1966.

11. Jean M. DeS. Howse and James L. Fitch, 'Effect of Parent Orientation in Sign Language on Communication Skills of Preschool Children', *Amer. Annals of the Deaf*, 117: 459-62, 1972.
12. Marshall S. Hester, 'Manual Communication' in *Report of the Proceedings of the International Congress on Education of the Deaf and of the Forty-First Meeting of American Instructors of the Deaf* (Washington: Government Printing Office, 1964), pp. 211-21.
13. Henry W. E. Klopping, 'Language Understanding of Deaf Students under Three Auditory-Visual Stimulus Conditions', *Amer. Annals of the Deaf*, 117: 389-96, 1972.
14. Stephen P. Quigley, *The Influence of Fingerspelling on the Development of Language, Communication, and Educational Achievement in Deaf Children* (Washington: Rehabilitation Services Administration, n.d.).
15. Stephen P. Quigley and D. Frisina, *Institutionalization and Psycho-Educational Development of Deaf Children* (Washington: Council for Exceptional Children, 1961).
16. Bernard T. Tervoort, 'Speech and Language Development in Early Childhood', *Teacher of the Deaf*, 62: 37-57, 1964 and Helmer R. Myklebust, *The Psychology of Deafness* (2nd ed., New York: Grune and Stratton, 1964).
17. Eugene Bergman, 'Autonomous and Unique Features of American Sign Language', *Amer. Annals of the Deaf*, 117: 20-24, 1972. See also, Donald F. Moores, 'Psycholinguistics and Deafness', *Amer. Annals of the Deaf*, 115: 37-48, 1970, and, Louis J. Fant, 'Comment: On Cracking the Language Barrier', *Amer. Annals of the Deaf*, 117: 365-67, 1972.

9. Problems confronting a priest in the pastoral service of the deaf in East Africa

P. Bergmann

INTRODUCTION

Being a priest who happens to be a teacher of the deaf and the manager of a school for the deaf at Tabora in East Africa (at 5° latitude and 37° longitude to be exact), I was asked to prepare a short paper on the above mentioned topic.

It is obvious however that East Africa is far larger than the space taken by one town in one of its countries: Tanzania. The deaf population is far more numerous too than the odd eighty children we have in our school and the 100 with whom I have had contact. The pastoral experience I have does not in any way cover the one supposed by the title of this paper. Therefore I will just mention some problems encountered by us in the religious educations of our deaf children and our approach to them, as a part of our pastoral service to the deaf in East Africa.

PROBLEMS ENCOUNTERED

The fact that we are the only school for the deaf in Tanzania, that Tanzania is a pluralistic Society and that not all denominations represented at our school are also represented in Tabora town, may count for some of the problems met with by us.

OUR SCHOOL – THE ONLY SCHOOL

To-date we are the only school for the deaf in Tanzania. Our school is a catholic school in as far as it was conceived by the late Msgr. J. C. van Overbeek and is run by the Archdiocese of Tabora. But not all of our children are catholic. The school is at the disposal of all deaf children of Tanzania and out of the 12 million inhabitants of Tanzania only about 1¹/₂ million are catholic.

It is not the aim of our school to make catholics of all the deaf of Tanzania, but to give them an opportunity of education equal to the one enjoyed by the non-handicapped citizens ... ut vitam habeant et abundantius habeant (St. John 10.10).

The deaf children are in need of education. We can satisfy that need. But it would neither be fair nor just to profit from this need (and which we alone can satisfy) to snatch the children away or alienate them from their parents. We catholics would not like it if other denominations profitted from our needs and took our children away. Moreover it would be ruinous to the education of the deaf if such a short-sighted policy was followed. The Government and other denominations would of necessity interfere.

Our obligation towards the children, the parents of various denominations and the country gives us therefore our first set of problems as far as the religious education of the children is concerned. We catholics are offering all of them a service, not setting a trap.

TANZANIA – A PLURALISTIC SOCIETY

Our pupils come from all over Tanzania. The conditions for admittance are that the children are deaf, of the correct age and do not suffer from other mental or physical disabilities which might hinder their education.

Tanzania is a large country – about 365,000 square miles. Tabora is situated pretty well in the centre. Some children have to travel over 400 miles before reaching the school, several even close to 1,000 miles.

Tanzania has many different religious denominations. Out of our 80 children only 34 are catholics. The others are christians or moslems, of various denominations, and a few have their ancestral religion. Not all the beliefs of each denomination are understood by us.

Tanzania's population is made up of very many tribes. At our school 36 are represented. It is clearly impossible for us to know the language, customs and pratices of all of them. At one time we had as many as 43 different tribes represented. It is hard to get a real picture of the children's home situation. Even if we know the tribe and denomination to which their parents belong, we still do not know anything about their practical adherence to it in daily life and consequently of the influence these factors have had on the child.

140

The variety of cultural and religious backgrounds of our children, combined with the great distances of the country, offer us therefore another set of problems as far as religious education is concerned.

REPRESENTATION OF RELIGIOUS DENOMINATIONS IN TOWN

Tabora has many and varied centres of worship. But even so, not all the denominations we have at our school have their representative in town.

Even if each and every denomination was represented in town, instruction difficulties would remain. Not everyone would be willing and able to teach our pupils due to the very special manner of approach needed and due to the very small number of children they would have to be contented with. This concise summary may give some idea of the problems encountered in securing for our deaf children a proper religious education. How then do we try to cope with our problems?

OUR APPROACH

When the child comes to school for the first time, preferably accompanied by one of the parents, we ask the parents to which religious denomination does the child belong and in the case of christians, to which Sunday Service to they wish him attend. We abide by their decision.

PRAYERS

In class we use informal prayers which can be said by all. We try to avoid all that looks specifically catholic in words and/or actions.

Catholics go to the parish church on Sundays, other Christians to the places indicated by their parents. Moslems go to the mosque on their feastdays.

INSTRUCTION

Religious instruction is given by the class teacher. It is always very general and restricted to our relation with God. If something specifi-

141

cally christian or catholic is treated, it is given to the ones to whom it concerns. Daily happenings, feasts of various denominations, sudden deaths, burials, etc., give plenty of subjects and ample scope for instruction.

Catholics are prepared for first communion and confirmation but then it is up to the parents during the holidays to see to it that the children receive these sacraments. Confessions are heard when the children request it.

CORRECT MORAL BEHAVIOUR

Training of this kind is most effectively given by insisting on correct behaviour in everyday life and in correcting the children when they do not conform to the norm set out, by showing them the harmful effects such behaviour can have on themselves.

Many of our children try to profit from their handicap. Being deaf they pretend they do not understand. Once they realise however, that we know their trick, most of them readily conform.

The older children have to look after the younger ones. It teaches them to think of others. The children have to do their own laundry, they have to look after the upkeep of the grounds, the cleaning of the classrooms etc. etc. It can be a remedy against laziness. These examples can be multiplied. Since we are with the children all day and they come in and out of our offices, they therefore feel quite free to ask all kinds of questions, some improper but some also which really trouble them.

It offers a golden opportunity to give them the proper outlook on life and teach them to accept and live with their handicap.

CONCLUSION

Until now we have not had any regular school leavers. It is hard for us to know what kind of problems they will present. A proper follow-up will be extremely hard to organise, due to the great distances involved.

Adults are also helped by us. The greatest difficulty they had was that of accepting their handicap. One youth comes back at regular intervals for a new supply of batteries for his hearingaid, the real reason is that he wants to discuss his problems with someone who may understand them and who takes the time to listen to him.

142

This brief paper may give some idea of the problems we encounter and the way in which we try to cope with them. We have just recently started and we are learning all the time. We will profit by knowing of the various kinds of pastoral services offered to the deaf in other countries and the manner in which they are administered.

10. Clubs for the deaf: experience of priests who are in the pastoral service of the deaf

D. O' Farrell

My fifteen years as a chaplain to the deaf have convinced me that Clubs for the deaf can play a very important part in the religious education of the deaf after they leave school. I would like to describe briefly some of the services and facilities available to Catholic deaf people in Scotland to help them live full christian lives. For the benefit of those who do not know Scotland it may help to give a few basic statistics. Scotland is approximately 30,000 square miles, about the same size as Ireland. It has a population of about 5 million. Scotland has its own Hierarchy of two Archbishops and ten bishops. There are eight dioceses. The Catholic population is about 800,000 but is very unevenly distributed. Croy, near Glasgow has a 95 % Catholic population. Glasgow has a 40 % Catholic population. Some towns of the East and North of Scotland would have less than 5 % of their population Catholic. The Catholic deaf population follows the same pattern. We have the names of over 400 deaf people in Glasgow. We only know of 300 other deaf people living in the rest of the country.

St. Vincent's Club for the Deaf, Glasgow, was formed to meet the social and religious needs of the past pupils of St. Vincent's School for the Deaf, Tollcross, Glasgow, the only Catholic school for the deaf in Scotland. A Sister of Charity, Sister Joseph Duff, devoted herself full time to this work in the 1930's. In 1949 Fr Dermot Sweeney, C.M. was appointed as the first chaplain to the deaf in Scotland. Backed by a committee of some of Glasgow's prominent citizens the work of the chaplain and the Sister of Charity was put on a firm legal and financial basis. Premises, consisting of a house and a hall, were given to the society for the deaf by the Archdiocese of Glasgow at a nominal rent. The Corporation of Glasgow recognised the social and welfare work done for the deaf by St Vincent's Club by giving an annual grant to the Club.

It is part of the role of the Club for the deaf to see that deaf people are brought into the life of the Church in the fullest possible way. To compensate for the loss experienced by the deaf when they attend Mass in their local churches and cannot hear a word spoken by the priest, we have a Mass in sign language on the first Sunday of the month. The Saturday before the first Sunday is an official confession night. Confessions are also heard before the Mass on the first Sunday of the month. The priests of the parishes in which deaf people live are glad to make use of the chaplain to the deaf in situations where communication is difficult and exact understanding is important. Instructing couples before marriage is one example. Instructing and receiving converts would be another example. Sometimes the chaplain is asked to Baptise the children of deaf parents. On occasions the chaplain brings Holy Communion to deaf people who are sick at home or in hospital. The chaplain is available for confessions and for spiritual advice in the Club at other times. Deaf people living up to 100 miles away have come for confession and advice. Every year a 'Retreat' is held in the Club. The retreat takes the form of Evening Mass, Sermon and Confessions on four days of a week. A chaplain to the deaf from England or Ireland is usually asked to give the retreat. A successful pre-marriage course for engaged deaf couples was organised this year. It was arranged with the co-operation of the Catholic Marriage Advisory Council in Glasgow. One young man travelled almost fifty miles in both directions each week to attend this course.

In Scotland, the welfare of the deaf is provided by nine voluntary societies for the deaf. These societies act as agents of the Local Authorities. This means that in Glasgow the Catholic deaf rely on St Vincent's Club for their social and recreational needs as well as their spiritual needs. Outside Glasgow the Catholic deaf usually go to their local club for recreation and for help with their material needs such as employment. This pattern is likely to change as Local Authorities begin to employ Social Workers for the deaf. The voluntary societies would then devote most of their attention to religious and recreational activities. In the meantime it is the aim of the Catholic Club for the Deaf to see that the spiritual needs of the deaf are not neglected and that the Catholic deaf are not condemned to a second-rate service as far as social welfare and recreation and further education is concerned.

One advantage of the present set-up already mentioned, is that the Catholic Club gets a substantial grant (£ 1,500) from the Corporation every year. From the religious point of view, it means that deaf people in need can be helped more comprehensively. In our social work for families and individuals religion is taken into account in diagnosing and finding solutions to the many complex problems presented to us. There is no question of insisting on attendance at Mass as a necessary condition for receiving help from our Club.

It is true that many of the aids to the religious education of the deaf provided by the Club for the deaf could, in theory, be provided by a chaplain and a Catholic Social Worker without a social Centre or Club for the deaf. In Scotland experience has shown that, at least in the past, without a club for the deaf these services would not be provided. The situation for Catholic deaf people living far from Glasgow is not satisfactory. Efforts are being made to form a national association for the Catholic deaf to bring pressure to bear on Church authorities to help these people. Special Masses for the deaf in other centres is one of the steps being considered. Another step which has been tried is the use of an interpreter at a public Sunday Mass to which the local deaf people have been invited. To date, the appointment of part-time chaplains to the deaf can hardly be considered a success. The parish commitments of the chaplains in Edinburgh and Motherwell made it too difficult for them to have the time and training necessary to be able to communicate freely with the deaf.

It is impossible to assess the pastoral effectiveness of a Club for the deaf. All the indications are that the atmosphere of the Club, the contact with a priest and a Sister of Charity are substantial helps to the spiritual lives of the deaf. The deaf attend Mass at least as regularly as their hearing counterparts. In my view, due partly to the Club for the deaf, their family life is stable. Perhaps the highest tribute to the spiritual effect of the Club and the Catholic School for the deaf was paid by the Presbyterian Welfare Worker for the Deaf from Paisley recently. In a conversation with me he said he thought the Catholic deaf were better than others at helping those with special needs. He was referring to the regular visits to hospitals and homes for the elderly by the younger and more active deaf to cheer up those who were lonely or chronically ill without any visitors.

146

11. Clubs for the deaf: experience of priests who are in the pastoral service of the deaf

J. Cleary

Father O'Farrell has already outlined the services to the deaf which are possible through a club. In Ireland these services are made available through St. Vincent's Club for the Deaf which is run in close co-operation with the schools for the deaf. Because of the lack of trained personnel to work with the deaf in the Club it is necessary for the Chaplain to depend very much on the teachers in the school who already have full time teaching responsibilities.

I am a Vincentian priest but my appointment as Chaplain to the Deaf is diocesan. Another priest has just been appointed but since he has not worked with the deaf before he will need a period of training. Besides being Chaplain to the Club I am also Chaplain to two large schools for the deaf, which have a total enrollment of 600 pupils. Recently the National Association for the Deaf which is a voluntary organisation made the services of a social worker available to the Club. We have excellent consistent voluntary help from members of the Legion of Mary. However we cannot provide a constructive service without more full time personnel.

The Club premises in Dublin were provided by the Catholic Institute for the Deaf which was founded in 1845 to provide educational facilities for the deaf in Ireland. An annual rent is paid to the Catholic Institute for the Deaf. The Club is run by a committee of deaf men and women of which I am Director. I provide supportive advice and guidance to the Committee without interfering with the actual running of the Club. The Club which caters for the full age range is extremely well run and is well attended. It has many and varied activities including the production of a newsletter. I would like to see the 'bridging'of services – more outside services being brought to the Club and likewise greater participation by the deaf in outside services. This will not be possible without further professional help which seems to be the greatest need of the Club at present.

A priest works as Chaplain to the Deaf in Cork and a priest and brother work for the deaf in Belfast but the deaf in the rest of Ireland have no such help. Due to the initiative of the National Association for the Deaf clubs have been formed recently in other parts of Ireland such as Tralee, Limerick, Waterford and Galway. They have good voluntary support in their own neighbourhood but as yet they have no pastoral service. We can only hope and pray that the situation will improve in the not too distant future.

12. Making the liturgy meaningful to the deaf

G. J. McGrath

INTRODUCTION

Among man's basic needs, is the need to find some meaning in his life. Gone are the days when man saw God in the Universe around him. This vision has been replaced by the workings of man; whether they be in the rockets and satellites, the bridges and apartment buildings, the electric guitar or the precise hands of the heart surgeon. These achievements and advances seem to spell out clearly that man by his own power, can create a heaven on earth. Yet at the very climax of this dream, at the very centre of this fragile optimism, disillusionment is setting in; as hard facts and a growing uneasiness indicate that this dream is becoming less and less meaningful.

Since even primitive times man has attempted to find meaning to his life by searching for a God. This, fundamentally, is what Liturgy is; 'man's attempt to give meaning to his life by relating it to the divinity'. It is the Christian belief that beyond this world and this life, there is a personal God who loves us; that we are called to co-operate with Him in his work, that through this co-operation with Christ we are destined for life everlasting. This intimate relationship to God glorifies our lives with a meaning so sublime, it can only be known by faith. This is the meaning of man's life 'that is celebrated and kept alive for all generations of mankind in the Christian Liturgy'.

Every generation of mankind needs contact with God. To the early Christians Christ among them was the sign of God's love. Because all generations need contact with God, Christ must be present in every age. God decided he would accomplish this by being present in the Liturgical celebrations of His Church. He is present in the sacraments so that when a man baptizes, it is really Christ Himself who baptizes. He is present in His word, since it is He Himself who speaks when the Holy Scriptures are read in the Church. He is present, finally, when the Church prays and sings, for He promised 'When two or three are gathered together for my sake, there am I in the midst of them'.

From this concept of the nature of Christian Liturgy a number of important consequences emerge:

a. Since the Liturgy is the action of Christ in His Church, the entire people of God are involved in it.
b. All Christians who by reason of their Baptism share in Christ's priesthood have both the right and the duty to share in the exercise of His priestly function.
c. The Liturgy is intended to celebrate and promote in the Christian community the meaning of our lives as Christians, that human life has final and eternal significance.

This means, quite unequivocally that full and active participation by all the people of God present at the celebration is necessary for the action of Christ to be properly accomplished. (May I digress a moment?) Merely wishing this will happen when the majority of the faithful present are mere spectators will not allow us to label it a Liturgical action. And please if you hear yourself saying 'but it's different with the deaf' or 'my children are multiply handicapped so . . .' then you have missed the point of the Liturgy. God knows who they are. You know who they are and the Church says '. . . it is the duty (of pastors) and that's you and me, also to ensure that the faithful take part, fully aware of what they are doing, actively engaged in the rite and enriched by its effects'. The Church does not say '. . .it is the duty of pastors also to ensure that the faithful – except those who are handicapped or except those who are illiterate – take part, fully aware of what they are doing, actively engaged in the rite and enriched by its effects'. If she did, she would fail to recognise the needs of many of the people of God.

'Bishops – Bells and Benediction'

As an epitome of the old Liturgy is reasonably accurate. More topical expressions of opinion (from which you might like to choose what appeals to you) go something like this.

'The chief function of Liturgy is to bring US divine life NOW' (Parsch). Liturgy is first and foremost concerned with the present. The past and future are only signposts of to-days outpouring of grace. The Constitution recalls that 'the Liturgy remains the central activity of the Church'. Dalmais in 'Mission and Witness' says 'The Liturgy is that action by which the Church as a social body, becomes aware of herself as she is established in the world'. Finally, the definition proclaimed with

150

dramatic single-mindedness by the Conciliar Fathers to bring out the inner reality of the Liturgy is –

God,
working through Christ,
active in the Church,
saving mankind.

A Matter of Attitudes

The feedback I got from the schools indicated that little is being done in most schools for the deaf. I'm not prepared to believe that this indicates a lack of interest in the Liturgy. But I do think it indicates in the cliche of the day a 'hang-up' on the Liturgy; a feeling that little can be done, except in the more obvious areas of Offertory processions, interpretative dancing and the like. Perhaps a few may identify with the story told by Fr. Sloyan in his book 'Worship in a New Key'.

'Once there was a tribe of primitive men who lived far up-river in the jungle, and who began to die in great numbers from the disease known as typhus. A health officer from the central government of the vast territory came to visit them. He shortly suspected the trouble, ran some tests with his field equipment, and then began to take the normal precautions.

'Calling the chief and the head men together he gave strict instructions from now on all the drinking water was to be boiled. He even gave a demonstration in the village square, where the most important business was carried on, of how this was to be done. Then he told the leaders to spread the word to all the heads of families and the women-folk. That night he rested easy for the first time in weeks.

'The next day, seven more tribesmen were reported dead; the day after that, four; the third day, nine. The reason was: no one was boiling his drinking water according to instructions. The doctor fumed. He pleaded. He threatened to bring the governor. He cried. Still no one would boil any water.

'You see, neither their fathers nor their fathers' fathers before them had ever boiled water. Their way, therefore, had to be right, and the health officer's way wrong. It was as simple as that'.

That is a tale of simple folk, you might say. It couldn't happen here. The sad fact is, though, that some of the local tribesmen are college graduates and a few have even completed seminary courses. They would not think of singing lustily at Mass or walking in procession or

151

looking straight in a fellow-parishioner's eyes, even if their lives depended on it.

Funny thing. It does. Eternal life hinges on our participation in the mystery of Christ's death and resurrection, and more alarming still so do the lives of our deaf boys and girls.

God I Offer You Me

I consider these next few thoughts the most important of this paper.

If God, the Sacraments, the Mass, the Church, Liturgy become *things* – you can forget about God. He just isn't there. God reveals Himself through the day by day events of each person's life interwoven with the lives of others. We must not continue to put the cart before the horse and introduce children prematurely to doctrinal matter and liturgical celebration. Real attitudes and experiences like speaking – listening – giving – changing – belonging – forgiving – playing – discovering – creating, are experiences the child celebrates naturally and they cannot be divorced from Liturgy. Let us call these celebrations liturgy with a small 'l'. Family birthdays, anniversaries, school patron or parish patron feast days are all opportunities for our children to become aware that the most ordinary happenings which occur as they live, work and play are the human materials from which their worship develops. Yet all these patterns of living are incomplete unless they reach their peak ultimately in Liturgy. Putting this another way, yet at the same time confirming the need for this Liturgy the church says, 'It (the Liturgy) is the summit . . . and the fount towards which the activity of the Church is directed'. (Art. 10)

The real 'stuff' of the Liturgy

If we are to understand the Liturgy at all, we must understand how we were redeemed because Vatican II describes the Liturgy as 'the activity through which the work of our redemption is exercised'.

To reveal Himself and His plan for our salvation the Son of God accommodated Himself to our way of acting and became one of us. He did not redeem us by acting as a pure spirit. He really entered our lives our human history and acted through His human nature.

Christ Himself is the Great Sacrament, the sign if you like, of the redeeming grace of God.

As the Glorified Lord, Christ wishes to continue to make present to men this redeeming grace, and once again he accommodates himself to the human way of acting. As men, we do not communicate with each

152

other on the spiritual level. We do not meet immediately on the level of thought, but we always find it necessary to externalise our thoughts so that another person will be put into contact with us. We use speech, gestures and even material objects which we press into our service. We use the powers of our bodies, pen and paper, telephone and gifts to express our thoughts and feelings to others. In other words in our dealings with others, we act through signs. Surely this approach, this explanation is both suitable and comprehensible to our deaf.

Christ acts in this way in the Liturgy. He could act directly upon us, but since we are creatures of flesh and blood he fits in with our way of acting and has many tangible means which serve to communicate himself and his saving reality to us.

We must be careful here. Many people feel that when we speak of sign in the Liturgy we are talking about something that is not a reality. There are signs which merely call our attention to something, which remind us if a fact, but which in no way make that reality present to us. We do use this type of reminding sign in the liturgy. For example, the incense can serve to remind us of prayer rising to God; statues to remind us of persons.

But there are also other types of sign in the Liturgy. The Eucharistic bread is a sign of the offering of Christ to us, but in and through that sign we know that the reality is communicated.

This is the kind of sign that we use most frequently in our ordinary human relationships. When we shake hands and greet another person we are giving him a sign of friendship, but in that very action our friendship is communicated. So in the Liturgy. The Constitution of the Liturgy reminds us that Christ is present in the signs of the Mass and Sacraments, and that he acts through them to communicate Himself to us.

Many Catholics are unhappy at the many recent changes in the Liturgy. Often this unhappiness arises because of a failure to see that the Liturgy is completely in the realm of signs. A sign of its nature is that which either leads to or conveys another reality. It is not an end in itself, but is a means to serve an end. If it fails to serve that end in the best possible way, then it should make way for another mode of expression which does. Some of the elements in the Liturgy have been given their meaning and value by Christ Himself and are therefore unchangeable, but many others are human expressions of the divine reality and therefore must be shaped to serve as the most transparent vehicle possible to convey Christ's activity to us on the one hand, and our response to God on the other.

There is another important consequence of the sign nature of the Liturgy. Just as the Church itself is not the end of Man but the means to lead him to full and final union with God, so also the liturgy is not celebrated for its own sake. Attendance at Mass, for example, is no guarantee of salvation, but in the Eucharistic celebration we can come into contact with Christ who is offering Himself to us through the Readings and the Eucharistic Bread. We must accept the offer which is aimed at leading us to make a personal response of love and dedication.

In the Liturgy we have a wonderful treasure. Christ offers Himself to us and we have the means to make our response. But there is nothing magical about the Liturgy. The signs may not be always perfect but much is being done to help us realise the reality that is being given to us, a reality that is calling us to act in a personal and vital way.

'Now to the Performance'

The stage is set, the lights are ready – now to the performance!

What can we *do*? And here I'm quite conscious of priorities.

We will be touching on Sacraments in general; on Baptism, Confirmation, Penance with special attention to the Eucharist in conjunction with the Mass, a few words on the Church Year, Scripture and Liturgical Dancing.

SACRAMENTS IN GENERAL

A brief statement and a suggested approach.

One of the ways of present theologians to Sacraments is that the celebration of a Sacrament is 'an event that is divinely charged with power of its own' to communicate grace to us. It is a grace laden event for us in our personal history but it depends on our personal dispositions. The Sacrament will not 'do the trick on its own'.

What approach do we take with our pupils to develop the dispositions necessary for an increase of grace through the Sacraments? O'Shea (The Christ Life) asks for an increase in involvement, in service. (We will be looking at this important question of service more deeply in relation to the Eucharist): an increase in the spirit of belonging to one another, and O'Shea goes on to ask, 'is there any such thing as grace without mission? Is there any such a thing as charity without service? Is there any such thing as love without belonging? Not if you

154

mean the Spirit of Christ. These ideas will develop a more practical bias as we deal with a few of the Sacraments on their own.

BAPTISM

'Baptism is the invitation of the new candidate into the service of this local servant community'.

The difficulty might be – Is this community (the parish or school) engaged in some service?

If you are anxious to get across the idea of Baptism (and you should be) a short 'mystery' play may appeal to you. There is a stage – in the centre a small swimming pool called the font of Baptism. The people of God are present and take part. The title of the play is 'The Pash of Christ'. One character is called on to take the part of Christ. Who, it doesn't matter. He is led to the water which symbolises death, led to the depths and immersed in it. He is Jesus Christ on the first Good Friday going down into the depths of His death. Then He is lifted up out of the water. He is Jesus Christ rising from the dead on Easter Sunday.

It has been suggested that there be an official Baptism ceremony in a big parish (or school) one Sunday a month, rather than any Sunday afternoon. This would bring home the idea of the presence of a community, worshipping and praying and receiving new members into the Church. Already there has been much work done on revising the rite and a special Baptismal Mass is being drawn up.

CONFIRMATION

In giving a little more attention as I'm going to, to Confirmation, I'm merely suggesting it is more functional for us as teachers. (By the way, generally in this paper I will refer to liturgical practices without mentioning the school concerned. You will pardon the mention of our school in regard to Confirmation. It would be difficult to relate what was done and maintain anonymity!)

Rather than deal with the many areas involved in this Sacrament of Confirmation, or in fact any sacrament, we decided to confine ourselves to dealing with a few of the more practical aspects. The core of the teaching, or the accent, was on the mission of service in which alone maturity can really be achieved. We explained, over a period

155

of four or five days the coming of age or initiation ceremony in the aboriginal tribes in Australia. How the young boys were only allowed help the women at home and not allowed work or hunt with the men or perform the ritual dances. At the right age the boy was 'stolen' from the woman and only after the initiation ceremony, which was circumcision or knocking out of front teeth or scarring chest or arms etc., was the boy allowed hunt with the men and *be of service* to this family, clan, horde, or tribe. The dramatization of this was very much enjoyed by the boys. The parallel with Confirmation was easily appreciated by them. By the way, it is interesting to note that in the new rite of Confirmation 'the intimate connection which this Sacrament has with the whole process of initiation is to be more clearly set forth'. (Art. 71 of the Const.)

By carefully choosing a wide variety of pictures depicting people helping others, we re-inforced this concept of service. We touched on the fear of the apostles, the reason for it, the effect of the coming of the Spirit, then paralleled this in their lives.

On the day of Confirmation we had the parents come to school. They had already followed our approach by letter. After a short further explanation we had lunch. At this, the parents continued their role of service to the boys and served them lunch. After Confirmation at the parish church, we returned to school and the boys served the parents afternoon tea They enjoyed this very much. The Council mentions the renewal of Baptismal vows before Confirmation as a way in which the connection with Baptism could be expressed. It also allows Confirmation to be given within Mass, which would certainly help to show how it prepares for the Eucharist.

A TIME FOR FORGIVING

A young mother once remarked to her parish priest, 'My child will never learn how to go to Confession. He can't remember the offences he commits at home; after a quick punishment, he forgets it in a minute'. We might do well to remember that remark! A child about eleven finds the process of forgiving rather difficult mainly because he is moving into the age of peer relationships. However, he slowly begins to experience the need to forgive and be forgiven. He is slowly realising that forgiveness requires unselfishness and a respect and understanding of others. The whole process of forgiving is developing.

I can't possibly go into the whole aspect of Confession, or as Karl

156

Rahner calls it the 'Liturgy of sinners'. Allow me to remind you that the Sacrament of Penance is only one small step in the overall sacramental process of blotting out sin. William Bekkers in his book 'God's people on the way' tells us that 'our concern must be to build a human foundation which will help children form their own conscience'. He goes on to say 'We must be careful not to "create" sins among adults, but even more care should be taken to prevent it happening when dealing with children'. We are told too, quite rightly that for Confession a child should have the language to express his own experience of good and evil and Chomsky reminds us that 'the limits of my language are the limits of my world'.

I hope that some one or other of the discussion groups will get onto this big question of Confession and come up with some thoughts on the setting for Confession, and implications of the following: a prepared list of sins; the record of failure of the deaf; inability of the deaf to apply the principles to other situations, insufficient evidence on our part to be able to determine moral age of the deaf.

No doubt some schools have already attempted to improve the understanding of the Sacrament for their pupils by communal celebration of freedom or forgiveness. Again it is important to recall that God reveals Himself through the day-by-day experiences of each person's life interwoven with the lives of others. Real experiences of their own or in the world around them cannot be divorced from Liturgy. So we must make use of the vital experiences of friendship, re-union of friends, loss of friends, freedom from jail or domination, et cetera, et cetera. Perhaps a celebration of their own Christic Redemption of being saved from the isolation of deafness by hearing-aids, language, their teachers!

One of the forms of communal service as done in one school for the deaf went like this. There was
1. Procession and/or hymn.
2. Liturgy of the word: Bible reading and/or filmstrip plus homily of conversion, forgiveness or some appropriate subject.
3. Communal examination of conscience: This was done in the form of a litany, thoughtfully and slowly, stressing the positive values of reconciliation while asking pardon for past failings; e.g.
   Jesus forgive me for being selfish.
   Jesus forgive me for being lazy.
   Jesus forgive me for being ungrateful.
4. Communal Act of Contrition. All say a brief act of contrition together, reading perhaps from a poster or overhead projector.

5. Prayer for forgiveness.
   Priest can then say the new sacramental 'absolution' prayers or their equivalent.
6. Communal Penance.
   As a sign of amendment all say together the Our Father or venerate the cross.
7. Sign of Peace: All exchange a handshake or other sign of friendship.
8. Private Confession and Sacramental absolution. Better to include this between 5 and 6 if the numbers going to Confession are small. As I said before – let's hope the subject is brought up in the discussion groups.

THE EUCHARIST

There is a practical and very real approach in the explanation of and adaptation of the Eucharist. St. John does not just return from the risen Christ to the crucified Christ. He goes back even further to an amazing scene; a scene which for sheer impact and message is reminiscent of that great moment in time – the Incarnation. Fr. Mollat of the Biblical Institute in Rome says 'The whole historical mission of Jesus and His whole message are concentrated in this single gesture of the washing of the feet as if He came into the world solely to perform it'. And isn't the Eucharist more than a Sacred sign? 'This is my Body *given up for you*'. 'This is my Blood *poured out for you*'. The new Commandment is the command to serve. As Jungmann tells us 'the emphasis now in the Mass is the community symbolism or more precisely, the meal-symbolism'. Have you ever looked at the celebration of a child's birthday party in relation to the Mass. The dialogue, the community, the singing – not saying, mind you – of Happy Birthday, the guests and their presents, the sharing of the birthday cake as they all assemble spontaneously around the cake to be cut! And there are still some who fail to recognise that Christ accommodates Himself to our human way of acting!

By the way don't fail to recognise that it is a *past event* – our birthday – that has meaning to us, that continues to influence us. We keep for instance photos of a wedding because they are a continual reminder of *a past event*. Because the Mass is the highlight of our Liturgy it would be well for me to detail some of the practices in some schools for the deaf.

158

Masses in classrooms. Masses for small groups – classes – around the table or altar.

Choice of themes for Masses. Masses nearer midday than early morning. Children seated around the table or altar. Entrance procession with all children participating by bringing something or playing. Penetential rite by kissing crucifix or by handshake of one another. The celebration of the word takes many forms, reading from projectors, simplified texts, film-strips depicting the readings, dramatisation.

One simple reading by the child.

Very brief readings and brief homily.

A helpful suggestion as the prayers of the Faithful is to use an epidiascope with contrasting pictures being presented one after the other.

Another way with slides, is to use two machines and show at the same time want and plenty, riches and poverty, love and hate, war and peace.

At the Offertory the usual procession of gifts or all the sacred objects used for the Mass, or again things connected with children's lives (including hearing-aids). A small money offering should be made occasionally by the seniors.

Children in some places make their own altar bread. The meal effect is more appreciated if unlevened bread is used.

The children can make gestures with their hands with the priest at the Offertory. At the Eucharistic prayer children can point to the elements at the Consecration as concelebrating priests do. In all of these activities children have recited the prayesr of the Mass or of simple hymns. At the Lord's prayer a few schools seem to have adopted the practice of joining hands in a big circle, priest included. The kiss of peace is given in various forms, usually it would seem by a handshake with the word 'Peace' or 'I'm your friend'.

At the Communion, children should be taught to say a good 'Amen' as also at the end of the Doxology. Some schools arrange short but successful pauses during Mass e.g. at Offertory, while the altar is being prepared. Some schools are attempting 'song', liturgical dancing, dramatisation, playing or rhythmical instruments and so on.

The question of what text to be used by deaf children is one that depends very much on the ability of each class or group to manage language. I would like to make two comments regarding the Mass that may initiate discussions.

One – the symbol of liturgical unity is best achieved when the local parishioners are grouped around their parish priest. In listening to and responding together to the Word and in sharing together in the meal, we, alienated and disagreeable individuals are being formed by Christ into a deep warm caring community of mature Christians. The point here being: all our children eventually attend Mass in their Parish!

The second reflection concerns the language of the Mass itself. Consider the following in relation to the language of the Mass for the deaf.

The more radical the structures get in a system (e.g. of Language) the more the system approximates to a new Language!

Basic to any Liturgy is some appreciation of the Bible or God's word. Let me begin with a very simple observation which should require no explanation.

Have you ever seen a young deaf child who still cannot read, clutch and carry about with him for days a letter from his family! Isn't this letter a sign that communicates? As a child reaches the age where a schema of historical facts and logical approaches are meaningful, he will be ready to see the kind of relations that are involved in the overall plan of the Old and New Testament.

To come to an understanding and fuller appreciation of the Bible a person must experience life in its symbolic realities. As 'A time for living' says, 'Unless a life is rich in human awareness the words of scripture will fall on unhearing ears'. It may help to recall for our children as a starting point some basic biblical notions.

Election – Covenant – Redemption. God's 'background of history'.

And, very briefly, they can be summarised at whatever length by each teacher.

Election: Israel, God's chosen nation – His personal love and mercy. We God's chosen and beloved children, through and in Christ.

Covenant: God's invitation to Israel to become His chosen people – Israel's obligation. God's faithfulness, God's invitation for us to become His sons.

Redemption: Worked out in the passion, death, resurrection, ascension of Christ. Or to look at it more succintly – salvation history as three fundamental phases of value – God's original vocation for man –

160

man's fall into sin and man's restoration in Christ. An early attitude to the Word of God by celebrating the Word at Mass, geographically apart from the Eucharist. During the day, facing the open book around towards the people after Mass, identifying a simple or apt phrase by picking it out with a light. Displaying the Bible reverently in the class room. Having solemn processions of the Book at start of Mass.

THE LITURGICAL DANCE

An expression of the inner prayer of the soul, expressed outwardly through the body. Man is not only spirit but flesh, and our Creator expects us to use the bodies He has endowed with beauty and grace.

Dancing is the entire body praising and praying to God. Fr. Lucien Diess does 'not see how dancing could be introduced during the Mass without doing violence to its structure'. There is however plenty of scope before or after Mass or during celebrations of the Word.

The following is a 'classic' programme for the celebration of the Word.
Entrance Rite
Organ or musical instruments
Entrance Hymn (Dancing)
Opening Blessing (Brief prayer)
The Word of God
Gradual Hymn – Dancing
Homily
Prayers
    Prayers of Faithful
    Prayers of President
    Our Father
Closing Rite
    Blessing or Closing Prayer
    Final Hymn – Dancing

'THE CHURCH YEAR'

This name, the official Liturgical books do not recognise. 'In liturgical parlance there really is no such expression'. It would be better to speak of Liturgical seasons or feastal seasons.

161

Some of the practices in this area of the Liturgy from some of the schools:

Advent. Making the advent wreath at craft lessons or at home with the family. Children's names were put in a hat to see what families would carry the wreaths on the four Sundays of Advent. The collect prayers were made up in the classroom or at home. They were put in the parish Sunday paper, and said as the wreath was handed to the priest. The Lector explained the meaning of the wreath during the procession.

Now rather quickly:

On *Sunday before Lent* a 'Mardi Gras' was held with children and some families at the pool site. There followed a barbecue and short concert by the children. Then on the *Eve of Ash Wednesday* the ALLELUIA was 'buried' in the church. Palms of previous Palm Sunday were also burnt.

On *Palm Sunday*, children carry palms at Offertory procession together with crown of thorns, purple cloak.

Holy Thursday in addition to the ceremonies (which some seniors attended) grapes, bread, sheafs of wheat, were carried at the Offertory.

Easter Sunday. New light, new life. At the Offertory Easter eggs, eggs, fern (new life), torches, candles, fluorescent lights were carried. The ALLELUIA was restored.

At the *Ascension* the crown, sceptre and orb (all explained, all made by children) were carried at the Offertory.

At *Pentecost,* the story was told and a group re-enacted this. It is a story the children enjoy more than you think. Small gifts for the family can be made at school.

One school experimented with liturgical dancing at night at a paraliturgy.

On the feast of *All Saints* in the parish of that name quite a big number of the children dressed up as different saints and the Lector spoke a couple of lines about each one as they walked up.

TRENDS IN THE LITURGY

I would like before closing this paper, to pass on to you some trends in the field of Liturgy. The application of these to the lives of the deaf I will not make. However it is evident that there will be greater opportunities for our deaf as the Liturgy becomes more and more 'man's attempt to give meaning to his life by relating it to the Divinity'.

162

We are of course always interested in those who foresee the future. As regards the Liturgy, while we cannot do this in detail some writers have attempted to give general outlines such as appeared in the magazine 'Worship' last year. This writer saw the forces of the electronic age at work shaping the Liturgy. We should be aware of these, and in our planning decide in what way we can use them to make the Liturgy more meaningful for the Deaf.

1. At present, responsibility for participation is on the shoulders of the laity as learning is on the student. In the future because conditions of groupings and mobility will be more flexible, the responsibility will be on the clergy and those who programme the celebration.

   This will create an entirely different situation to what we have today.

2. Greater variety of liturgical expression and form will be developed, mainly because the electric media will decentralize and create a dislike for uniformity. There will be a greater interest in forms of prayer which, while they form a close bond with official sacramental expression, provide a flexibility and possibility for creativity and innovation with which sacramental celebration can be enriched. This will also include the devotional and prayer life in the Church which will take on greater importance. Service will be created over which a Deacon or other person (like a teacher!) can preside.

3. The fact that we are restoring the main traditional lines of worship based on the apostolic tradition is a proof that we are involved in a new liturgical medium under electronic age conditions. For a new medium will first make use of older forms until it is competent to be creative in contemporary modes.

4. Creative and intelligent innovation will be welcome. This transition will be achieved by allowing the more intelligent and creative to innovate and experiment, and so help create a healthy new situation.

5. Liturgy in the future will cease to be presented in the uniform package. Congregations will develop at their own pace. Sunday celebrations will differ in a variety of styles. The 'floating parish' will continue to blur the rigid concept of the traditional territorial parish boundary. Yet eventually this very 'movement' will enhance traditional parish celebrations.

6. We will begin to look on liturgy something like radar detecting changes that can be expected in Church life, and this will give us advance warning to prepare for their impact. Like environment or day-by-day experiences, liturgy will be used more and more as a

'teaching machine' and will become the major factor of religious education for all Christians.

While my final words are not a summary of what I have said, they are a conclusion in the strict sense of the word. I will state two aims and two solutions.

a. Our efforts have to be towards crystallising the growth of a child's experiences in dynamic 'epiphanies' of self, others and God.

The solution is through an approach in which the day-to-day happenings and the people of a child's life are related and identified as experiences of faith. The very responses to these happenings and relationships which bring him to maturity and insure his development as a person are really what stimulate his religious development.

b. Hoffinger reminds us that 'our first and final task is to give our pupils a very great and very real idea of God their Father'.

Perhaps I am oversimplifying the solution but perhaps too our present approach needs simplifying! Religious education – what this Conference is all about – has to be a concrete, living thing. God's message of redemption is related by twin instruments. Scripture and Liturgy. That is, God's word and God's action.

Finally, two thoughts. We, you and I, are special. We are the instruments God has chosen. We have the privilege of manifesting the sublime meaning of human existence to these special children of His. We must not lose heart in our efforts. We must daily accept the challenge. More importantly, the Liturgy must become fully meaningful to us if we are to communicate it to others – and that has been the primary aim of this paper – but we dare not lose sight of the fact that the Liturgy is the action of Christ and has power to achieve its goal. It is also the action of the people of God and as such we are able to join with Christ in making this goal a reality.

Amen

QUESTIONS AND ANSWERS

Question
Is the simplified liturgy suitable for deaf children? By LITURGY we mean,
Liturgy in a very broad way.

Answer
By all means, I was told by Father Herman Schmidt S.J. who was on
the Commission for Liturgy and at present stationed at Gregorian
University, Rome, that he feels that experiments should be made by
teachers, like ourselves, with our own school children. It would also be
an advantage to have the approval of the Bishop for this experimenta-
tion. In most cases, the Bishop would have to be helped to understand
the communication problems of deaf children.

Question
May deaf children by the nature of their handicap be admitted to First
Communion before Confession?

Answer
We are not allowed to do this at present in our Diocese in Sydney.
This can present a problem to deaf children because of their retardation in language development. I would be entirely behind the practice
where deaf children would receive the Body of Christ before there was
any idea of their asking for forgiveness for a sin.

Question
At what levels do you prepare children for the reception of the Sacraments, and how long does this preparation take?

Answer
To date, I think they have been about nine years of age. There have
been a couple of eight-year-olds, who have made their First Communion. I think we would be more inclined to move this level down, as
standards are generally improving. How long it takes, depends on the
individual, and also on the teacher. If it is a question of First Holy
Communion, I feel that nothing but the identification of Who they are
receiving, as distinct from what they are not receiving, is all that is
necessary.

Question

You compare education to symbolic thinking. You mention also the lack of imagination and creativity. Could you give some hints as to how to bring deaf children towards better symbolic thinking?

Answer

I would like to feel that I could answer this question much more fully than I can. I think it is a very important area. When it comes to Liturgy, this appreciation of symbols and signs is the 'grass roots' of the matter. This is the way Christ is communicating with us at present in this form, and for that reason, it is immensely important. A lot of work is being done I am sure in many of the schools in each area, certainly in schools in Australia. The idea of 'light' is being developed by children being put in dark rooms for periods together as a class, and light being slowly or suddenly let in. They do drawings on black paper and then get the idea of light coming into this paper from the back. The idea of being out on a cold night and light being used to warm them – this whole idea of what light can do and what light means to us in all its forms, whether it be the florescent light, or the light of a candle, or the light of a big fire; what light has done to ship-wrecked people or people during the war – all these ideas bring out the symbolism of light and the same idea applies, I suppose to life. Some of the schools would spend three of four weeks with hearing children developing the idea of bread – you know, right back from where it come from, how it grows, what it means to us, what it does to us when we eat Bread; what life, what strength it develops in us. I am sure these ideas of light and warmth and life and food have many possibilities of development. It is something we have not looked sufficiently at, in our school, and I would say if there is to be any priority in the area of liturgy it must be on this development of symbol and sign.

Question

Please enlarge on the use of the liturgy as an instrument of teaching.

Answer

The human dimension and the religious dimension are not separate entities. I think if we keep this in mind anything that we do is meaningful and is part of their celebration. In my paper, I have used the word liturgy with a small 'l' to refer to anniversaries and birthdays. Father Schmidt, already referred to, would not agree with this. In this context, he would use Liturgy with a capital 'L' especially for instance

166

when a birthday is celebrated in the class-room. For him, this is LITURGY. This is the children's celebration. They become sensitive to the religious dimension of this in so far as the teacher is there and there is some religious dimension within this. If it is not, then there is a carry-over later on. The mention of 'as an instrument of teaching' I think that this could be explained by beginning for instance when a advent wreath is made, at the craft lesson, or at home with the family. Children's names are put in a hat to see what families carry the wreath on the four Sundays of Advent. The prayers are made up in the class-room or at home and appear in the parish Sunday paper. These prayers are said as the wreath is handed to the priest, and the Lector or the priest explains the meaning of the wreath during the procession. Palm Sunday is rather obvious. The whole idea of Palm Sunday can be visualised through liturgical practice or carrying the psalms at the Offertory procession together with the crown of thorns and the purple cloak. At the Offertory procession on Easter Sunday there would be an Easter Egg, a new fern which is an indication of new life. Torches, candles, florescent lights are also carried, and a particular 'Alleluia' which in some places was buried or put aside during this period, is restored again. And this to me seems almost sufficient to explain what is meant by Easter. And this I think, was in the context that I referrred to the liturgy being a possibility for teaching practically all of doctrine.

Question
How can we make sure that the liturgy is really meaningful to the deaf?

Answer
I did mention the idea of the human dimension and the religious dimension not being separate entities. I suppose that it is slightly off the topic of liturgy, but you know how the things that happen every-day to children are really the things that have meaning for them. In the morning before school, we usually take the children to a room, and whatever topical might have happened – for instance if the death of the three Russian cosmonauts was the talk amongst them, this was what concerned them. They had been following their activities, and we tried to get them not to think about this particular aspect. We might say to them 'You heard in the news, or saw in the news that these three Russian cosmonauts were found dead in the capsule. Well, we must not just think of these men now, we have to think of their families, of the wives and the children they have left at home, how they must feel'. We speak to the children too about the bravery of these

167

men, the service they have given to their fellow-men, and then after some explanation, whatever it might be, the teacher would perhaps stand up in front of the children, with eyes closed and then make a short prayer that the children would watch, not repeat themselves, but would watch. We would thank God our Father for such men as these, for how they have served people. I too am expected to serve people, and that by loving the people around me I am going to show how I love God, or God my Father. We mentioned things like this – and these were possibilities for a kind of worship and I am sure I am inclined now to put all of this in the realm of Liturgy, whereas I would not have, before I met Fr. Schmidt.

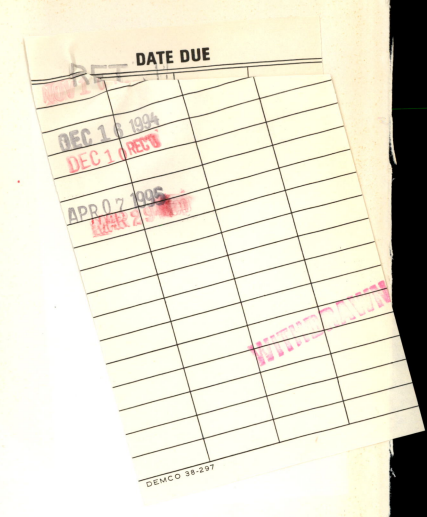